Marriage in *Motion*

Marriage in
Motion

*The Natural Ebb and Flow
of Lasting Relationships*

RICHARD STANTON SCHWARTZ
JACQUELINE OLDS

DA CAPO PRESS
A Member of the Perseus Books Group

Library of Congress Cataloging-in-Publication Data is available

ISBN 0-7382-0830-2

Da Capo Press is a member of the Perseus Books Group
Visit us on the World Wide Web at www.dacapopress.com

Da Capo Press books are available at special discounts for bulk purchases in the U.S. by corporations, institutions, and other organizations. For more information, please contact the Special Markets Department at the Perseus Books Group, 11 Cambridge Center, Cambridge, MA 02142, or call (617) 252-5298.

Cover design by Steven Cooley
Jacket photograph " Craig Aurness/ CORBIS
Text design by Jeff Williams
Set in 11-point Goudy by Perseus Publishing Services

First printing, August 2000
First paperback printing, August 2002

6 7 8 9 10—06 05

For our parents and our children

Contents

Authors' Note

The individuals and couples who appear in this book are real. We have altered circumstances and details to disguise their identities. We apologize for the inadequacy of our portrayals. The use of real stories to illustrate our ideas inevitably required us to present oversimplified versions of richly complex lives, each of which deserves a book of its own.

Acknowledgments

We would like to thank the many people—colleagues, friends, and relatives—who listened to, encouraged, and challenged our emerging ideas about lasting relationships. We are particularly grateful to those who read early drafts of this book and gave us at least some of the criticism we needed to improve it: Maggie and Craig McEwen, Adrian and Christine Slywotsky, and Nancy Murray. Other friends who gave us hope and advice include Michael Miller, Diane Canning, Carol Sacerdote, Alexandra Helper, Hubert Murray, Kate and Ken Cohen, and Melinda Brooks. Family members who tolerantly listened to our worries and provided important editorial advice include Nickie Olds, Doris Schwartz, and (our tolerant children) Nate and Sarah Schwartz. Our agent Carolyn Krupp was always a reliable source of support and good sense. Finally, we are incredibly appreciative of the responsive kindness and intelligence of our editor at Perseus, Marnie Cochran.

Introduction
Preserving Love

The heart is saturated with love as if [with] a divine salt which preserves it: that is what makes possible . . . the freshness of loves which have lasted a long time. Love embalms.

Victor Hugo, *The Man Who Laughed*

And the self is set free, for the moment, from the constant pressure of change.

Penelope Fitzgerald, *The Blue Flower*

At a small neighborhood restaurant, one of us met an old college roommate for lunch. Carl was looking forward to a week's vacation in Nova Scotia with his wife. He wanted to explain why the time together, free from their regular routines and responsibilities, seemed to matter so much:

When Louise gets busy and has meetings out three nights in a week, and I'm caught up in a project and working late, by the end of the week—I know it shouldn't happen so quickly—but she begins to be in a world where I no longer have ready access to her mind, even though we've been together for so long.

His words eloquently capture the tug-of-war between work and love in modern life, but they also point to a more fundamental pattern of ebb and flow that shapes all lasting relationships. There is a tidelike movement at the very heart of intimacy, a natural alternation of closeness and distance that either creates a sustaining rhythm of reconnection or, if misunderstood, drags two people apart. We will present a realistic yet hopeful picture of lasting relationships based on this knowledge, but first we must confront the dreams that cloud our vision.

Consider the apologies embedded in Carl's words. "I know it shouldn't happen so quickly." "Even though we've been together for so long." Here he is, talking to an old friend about a perfectly reasonable reaction, and yet he conveys a hint of embarrassment, a suggestion that things are not quite as they should be. He holds on to a notion of a more stable and enduring connection that would not be so sensitive to the pressures of everyday life. By that hidden measure, his own marriage falls short.

A Glance at Our Romantic Myths

For most of us, there is a startling and painful divergence between the images of intimacy that we long for and the experiences of closeness that we actually have. Over the ages, we have celebrated love, friendship, and family ties that remain fixed and constant though surrounded by change, bonds that buffer us against the painful transience of lesser relationships and ultimately of life itself. *Undying* love and *constant* friendship are the phrases that define our hopes and ward off our fears. These hopes may be mocked by cynics and seem to disappear for a while, but even cynicism must give way to our powerful longings for closeness.

It is easy to ridicule the fanciful hyperbole that these longings have spawned. We create industries to market our romantic metaphors back to us. A recent advertisement optimistically offered "A genuine 12" long-stem rose preserved & dipped in 24K gold. Like your love & commitment, it will last forever."

Though a bit crass, the ad simply seeks to profit from the undeniable power and beauty that images of changeless devotion have achieved in the hands of more successful poets.

A stroll through the psychology and self-help sections of most bookstores might seem to suggest a transformation of these romantic ideals, but it is at most a minor correction. The concept of "development over the life span," a view of adulthood as a process of change, entered modern psychology in the 1950s[1] and has taken firm hold of our imagination. The result is a new romantic myth, now common in books and columns offering advice on marriage, in which two people grow and change as individuals while holding the bond between them constant.

Yet a moment's honest reflection, even in the best of marriages and friendships, will confirm a simple though troubling observation: people are almost always moving closer together or further apart. When two people are moving toward each other, they take pleasure in the discovery and unfolding of another person. At its best, it is a joyful movement, filled with wonder. When the process of unfolding ends, rather than a sense of something gained for good, there is a feeling of loss, of something missing. If they try to hold the relationship static, to fix the distance between them and keep it constant, what was once a joyous connection begins to feel tense and unnatural. More often, a sense of loss or disappointment, usually unnoticed and unnamed, begins a drift apart.

When we describe this process to others, almost no one is completely surprised. Often there is a sense of recognition and, along with it, puzzlement that something so intuitively true is so regularly lost behind the haze of our expectations and myths. So before we begin to explore the implications of tidal drift in relationships, we need to understand the hold that the romantic ideal of intimacy retains over our lives. We must face the power of an image of "embalmed" closeness that, once gained, is either fixed and unchanging or totally and catastrophically shattered.

Everyone longs to escape from the troubling and often painful shifts in our real experiences of closeness. When we are happy, we naturally want our happiness to last. The constancy in our marriage vows—for better for worse, for richer for poorer, in sickness and in health, . . . till death do us part—portrays a steadiness of devotion and support extending through time and change. Yet Victor Hugo and Penelope Fitzgerald, in passages taken from novels written more than a century apart, suggest a more magical goal—a state of timelessness where decay is banished by the divine preserving salt of love. Despite wedding vows that acknowledge the inevitability of death, our not-so-secret wish is to escape from the unyielding flow of time that carries us steadily toward death and decay. "Happily ever after" is beyond time and change. At its most extreme, our vision of unchanging love offers us an apparent respite from the transience of life itself.

Hugo's language also reveals a paradox that is at the very heart of our romantic longings. In our wish to preserve the freshness of love and friendship, we risk becoming embalmers who create an illusion of life. Many of our most cherished love stories teach us that one of the only allies we have in this enterprise is, ironically, death itself. Probably the most pervasive archetype of romantic love in our culture is the story of Romeo and Juliet, where an early death preserves forever the freshness and constancy of their love. The twelfth-century legend of Tristan and Iseult, the original embodiment of the medieval ideal of courtly love, also portrays lovers captured in eternal, unchanging purity by death. Having unknowingly shared a love potion just before Iseult's marriage to King Mark of Cornwall, their love can neither be extinguished nor sanctified. It can only be frozen in its perfection by death. The love of Romeo and Juliet was blocked by ancient hatreds, that of Tristan and Iseult by their shared allegiance to Iseult's husband. For both pairs of lovers, however, there was no possibility that movement or change could be anything but catastrophic. When we compare the crystalline perfection of their romance to our own lives of disorderly change, we learn that time itself is the enemy of love.

In his sonnets, Shakespeare returns again and again to his horror of that enemy—"devouring time." He portrays its workings with power and terrible clarity, not unlike the Zen exercise in which one meditates on the decomposition of one's own body after death. We turn away from these images, almost instinctively, with dread. One place we regularly turn is to our faith in love as a divine salt that preserves the heart and our youth. Shakespeare, of course, also knows that his poetry can conquer time:

> Yet do thy worst, old time; despite thy wrong
> My love shall in my verse ever live young.[2]

Since most of us wisely lack similar faith in our own poetic powers, our efforts to deny the flow of time periodically collapse in the face of reality or are shattered by the grim visions of individuals who would strip us of illusions. That tough-minded enterprise has been embraced enthusiastically by a wide range of modern writers, artists, and filmmakers. Yet romantic dreams of love somehow survive their frequent literary death notices.

The modern Western romantic ideal is rooted in the concept of courtly love, which evolved in medieval Europe. The originator of that elevated tradition is believed to be William IX, Count of Poitier and Duke of Aquitaine, a worldly and licentious nobleman whose ribald songs celebrated his sexual adventures. Gradually his poetry changed. It began to express a pure and mystical longing for an idealized Unknown Lady, in whose service he would become that which was most noble within him. The rake was reborn as a romantic. And the pendulum continues to swing (as it always has) from worldly cynicism to romantic dreams and back again, oscillating slowly for cultures, more quickly for individuals, reflecting (as we will discuss later) the paired antithetical strivings for security and autonomy that seem basic to human nature. In this ancient cycle, romantic longings are periodically shattered by a cynical disillusionment which eventually gives way again to our romantic longings.

The image of oscillation, however, introduces an alternate model of stability that is based on movement rather than fixed distances. A basic tenet of engineering is that it is easier to create a stable system by constraining motion than by abolishing it. A standard example from nature is the tree that sways in high winds but would crack if it were more rigid, a design that has been adapted to such unlikely man-made constructions as massive skyscrapers. On the ground, the customary cracks in sidewalks serve the same function, allowing enough movement through seasonal changes of temperature, through freezes and thaws, to prevent shattering.

As Constant as the Tides

There is remarkable stability over time in physical systems that "give" enough but not too much, whether on the scale of molecules or heavenly bodies. The ebb and flow of the tides is one such system, the oceans responding with limited motion to the movements of the earth and the moon. The tides have been a time-honored symbol of the stability that can arise from constant motion. Tidal drift is a particularly apt metaphor to extend a model of dynamic stability from physical systems to relationships. Although tides are a global phenomenon, their local flow and the particular magnitude of their rise and fall is shaped by the idiosyncrasies of the local shoreline. Of course, local geography is itself reshaped over time by the tides in a complex interplay that is both generally predictable and completely surprising.

The drifts we will describe in human relationships, in friendships and in families as well as in romance, are very much like the tides. They ebb and flow predictably, yet their eddies and currents are unique to each relationship. And like the tides, acting quietly over time, they can transform the most resolute character. These shifts are not signals of catastrophic change, yet they can be dangerous if unnoticed or misunderstood. Two people may drift so far apart that the effort of return seems to require more energy than they can manage. They may misinterpret the periodic lessening of closeness and, in a panic, do something to shatter the relationship out of the misplaced fear that it is already ending.

We begin to see the potential destructiveness embedded in our otherwise inspirational romantic ideal. It leads people to damaging misinterpretations of natural developments and catastrophic responses to noncatastrophic events. If love is timeless, then any variation over time in our fascination or sense of closeness with a lover must mean that we are not in love. If true friendship is constant and steady, then a friend who rebuffs us while absorbed in something else is no friend. If a happy marriage means one where ardor and interest never waver, then a temporary drift further apart is grounds for divorce.

The tendency to see the ordinary ebb and flow of relationships as evidence of "irreconcilable differences" is even greater among the rapidly growing group of adults who have seen their parents' marriages end in divorce. Powerful personal experience leads them to mistrust the resiliency of relationships, to scrutinize their own bonds for signs of impending disaster and, in fear and self-protection, to believe they have found those signs in the smallest departures from their romantic ideals. Paradoxically, although the shattering of their parents' marriage makes them more cynical and "worldly," it also leaves them even more tyrannized by our idealized depictions of love. They are less able to tolerate the natural ebb and flow of all relationships.

In the following chapters, we will describe an alternative model of relationships that is both more realistic and more hopeful. It is the approach of the engineer who designs a system with enough give to keep it from cracking under ordinary stresses and strains, but not so much give that it simply comes apart. It is the approach of the naturalist at the seashore who comfortably anticipates the movement of the tides, but still keeps a watchful eye out for storms that can turn the usually benign ebb and flow into a genuine threat.

We offer these ideas at a time when hopefulness about sustaining a lasting and loving relationship is itself at a low ebb, a conclusion drawn from an extensive review of available attitude surveys and Census Bureau data in the latest report from the Rutgers University National Marriage Project.[3] In the words of the project's codirector Barbara Dafoe Whitehead, "Young people today want successful marriages, but they are increasingly anxious and pessimistic about their chances for achieving that goal."[4] A better understanding of the natural ebbs and flows in intimacy can dramatically improve their chances.

Of course, there are also hazards in the use of extended metaphors. Marriages are not seashores. If we get carried away by our imagery, we may begin to distort our picture of relationships rather than illuminating it. With that caution, we still hope to provide a new way of looking at close relationships, one that brings into sharp relief important but neglected aspects of their natural history. Although our discussion will often focus on marriage, it "applies equally well to all central adult relationships, including enduring heterosexual and homosexual alliances, deep friendships, and other dyadic relationships that form life's crucial context,"[5] to borrow a phrase from an article on marriage and individual well-being. We believe that our perspective has practical importance. It offers couples both a general framework and specific strategies to stabilize relationships within a culture that, despite its romantic myths, often provides little real support for long-term commitments.

Our descriptions may seem less scientific than precise measurements of closeness in relationships made with an exciting new technology, perhaps an ebb-and-flowmeter. Let us remember, however, that closeness itself is just a spatial metaphor for an essential human experience that we have no better way to describe. In a recent radio interview, the eminent psychology researcher Jerome Kagan observed that, alongside today's emphasis on formal research, there is an important role for "reflective commonsense." We hope that this book provides some of it.

What we cannot provide is something most couples would understandably want—the equivalent of a tide chart for relationships that predicts precisely when the highs and lows will occur. That would carry our metaphor too far. Closeness will inevitably ebb and flow but the pattern will be unique to each couple. It would be wonderfully comforting to have a time line of intimacy to paste on the wall or perhaps a *Farmer's Almanac* for marriage ("In the eighteenth month, passion will temporarily recede . . . "), but no reliable guide exists. Longitudinal studies of marriage have simply not delineated the kind of predictable developmental sequence that is present (at least to some degree) in individuals. If we tried to write a marital equivalent of *Passages*, Gail Sheehy's famous guide to the stages of adult life, we would only replace the old romantic myth with a more modern developmental myth. In fact, we suspect that hidden behind the search for a predictable developmental model of marriage is the same longing for certainty that makes us cling so tightly to the romantic ideal.

Closeness in a relationship will inevitably ebb and flow, but such movements will have a life of their own that do not necessarily correspond to the events that we commonly use to mark our progress through life—a wedding, the birth or departure of a child, success or failure at work. To anchor our discussion of a somewhat elusive phenomenon in recognizable situations, however, we will also look at these significant moments in a couple's life and see how they interact with the tidal drifts, how they sometimes shift the tides and are always complicated by them, and how an understanding of the rhythms of intimacy can help a couple to pass these milestones and remain together.

1

Tidal Drift

Charting the Course of Real Romance

Several days after giving a talk about closeness in psychotherapy, one of us received the following note from a colleague: "I had a talk with Matthew [age four] about your presentation on closeness. He said, 'What is closeness?' I said, 'Closeness between people.' He said, 'Like standing near each other?'"

Young Matthew got it right. Closeness between people *is* like standing near each other. For complicated reasons, the best language we have to describe human relationships is a language of spatial metaphors. We therefore begin with a simple metaphorical observation: in any personal relationship, at any point in time, two people are either moving closer together or further apart. There is no other real-world alternative. When two bodies separated in space are human bodies, the distance between them is always changing. Sometimes we believe that we have reached a motionless state, a love or friendship that is fixed and constant, but that impression is an illusion shaped by our fears and our desires.[1]

A joyful sense of intimacy does not come from static closeness but from movement toward each other, from the progressive discovery of another person, from a wondrous sense of unfolding and unveiling. Familiarity is, of course, an essential element of closeness, but what matters most is the sense of *growing* familiarity. When we no longer feel that we know the other just a little bit better today than yesterday, or at least a little better this year than last, then familiarity does indeed begin to breed contempt. Or at least complacency.

Sadly, closeness attained begins a movement apart. Often, it begins with a blessed sense of comfort and security that leads each person to take each other and the relationship for granted, to be inattentive and no longer curious about the other. But it is not just complacency that turns the tide; there is also a profound sense of loss. The process of moving closer to each other, with all its excitement and wonder, is exactly what has been lost. And so a sadness and regret enters the relationship, usually unnamed because it is so discordant with our romantic ideals, and a subtle drift apart begins.

Many years ago, an Indian woman told us that only an arranged marriage is truly romantic since the precious discovery of one's spouse becomes part of the marriage itself. She was perplexed by Western marriages that seem to begin just when the process of unfolding has ended. We think she understood something about the turning of the tides, but perhaps not their regular ebb and flow. A lover or a spouse who begins to drift away does not inevitably keep drifting off forever. Sometimes there is a spontaneous reawakening, a remembering of the other, a reaching out for what seems to be slipping away that not only reestablishes the old connection but recaptures the sense of movement toward each other and begins a new cycle of progressive closeness. More often, one member of the couple functions as a "distance alarm," consciously or unconsciously monitoring the ebbs and flows of the relationship and precipitating a crisis of reengagement when the drift apart has gone on too long. That alarm function is crucial to long-term relationships even though the partner who functions as the alarm is often misunderstood and treated like an irritating car alarm on a city street that is both cursed and ignored. Yet even in our era of high divorce rates, these to-and-fro movements of intimate relationships have a powerful stability.

In the Introduction, we gave examples of a range of physical systems, both natural and man-made, that achieve dynamic stability by limiting expected motion rather than trying to abolish it. In most situations, it is simply a safer and more reliable way to build something that will last. The approach works for "engineering" relationships as well. If there is too much rigidity as the tides of intimacy rise and fall, the relationship will either be shattered by the inevitable motion or, with no movement at all, become lifeless. If there is no resistance to movement apart, then there is only the illusion of a bond and the slightest motion will carry someone off for good. The challenge to the engineer is to get the amount of resistance right, to set an alarm system with just the right sensitivity. Somehow (and we will examine how), many couples do get it right and the natural ebbs and flows of intimacy are experienced as a powerful but not disruptive force in their lives together. Many couples do not, however, and normal rhythms become catastrophic events that flood a relationship with misunderstanding, disappointment, anger, and fear.

Here is a curious fact. Our description of tidal drift in relationships is, in some ways, obvious. It seems like something that everybody knows. It may be central to our earliest social experiences—even infants create cycles of intensity in their engagement with caregivers by making and breaking eye contact.[2] If it is so obvious, then, why is it so often and so catastrophically misunderstood? Part of the reason is the stories of love that shape our expectations, the romantic myth that was examined in more detail in the Introduction. The path to true love will be arduous and daunting, but love once attained burns with a constant flame. Or in the tragic version of the romantic myth, the flame is snuffed out or simply dies away and its loss is bitterly mourned. What, then, are we to make of it when we reach the peak and, instead of dwelling on the mountaintop in bliss, find ourselves going down the other side? Like the famous bear who came over the mountain, we just do not seem to understand the terrain. We think that in true love, there must be just one mountain. If we are going down, we must be living the tragic version of romance, or perhaps it was never love at all. We turn away. We lose hope. We begin to search for a new love story with someone else, hoping that the next love will last. We forget that it is the ebb and flow of love that lasts.

Sailing Away on an Ordinary Tide

Jennifer Sorenz was in her third year of law school when she felt the tide turning. She had met her husband in college. Their first few dates were like many she had before, but then something about Harold captured her curiosity. There was a feeling of wonder and excitement they shared as they each explored what the other was *really* like. Their romance, courtship, and marriage were at times turbulent, but Jennifer never lost the sense that their overall movement was toward each other until the last few months. She and Harold felt extremely comfortable with each other but their comfort did not hold her attention. Instead, her lively curiosity was focused on her final studies in law school, her emerging sense of mastery of a previously daunting field, and her career plans in a world far removed from Harold's graduate work in physics. Naturally, there was a fellow law student who shared her interests and anxieties. She and Robert spent increasingly long hours discussing their shared concerns over coffee. An undercurrent of flirting and sexual tension began to rise closer to the surface. At the same time, she experienced a growing sense of estrangement from her husband. Feeling that she was on the verge of an affair, Jennifer was both excited and appalled. She "realized" that she must no longer love Harold or she could not possibly be feeling the way that she did. Out of a sense of fairness to Harold, she announced that she must leave him. She proceeded to set in motion their eventual divorce.

Jennifer's devotion to the romantic ideal led her to mislabel the predictable and ordinary shifts in closeness over the course of a marriage as proof of a terrible estrangement. She quickly concluded that the marriage was irretrievably flawed. In a time of easy divorce, that perception is often all it takes to end a marriage. Yet the "problem" actually grew out of Jennifer and Harold's success as a couple—their sense of knowing each other so well, the closeness that let Jennifer feel safe and comfortable in a relationship for the first time in her life. That safety and comfort allowed her to relax her guard and become intensely involved in her studies, something she never had done in college when all her curiosity was centered on Harold. A temporary drift apart might have enriched not only Jennifer's life but Jennifer and Harold's life together, if only it had triggered an effort to reengage each other rather than a catastrophic blowing up of the marriage. They might have caught the tide of a new movement toward each other if they had recognized their drift apart as a natural phase in their intimacy instead of a crushing personal failure.

A Core of Sadness

A story of love or friendship as a cycle of closeness and distance is simultaneously a hopeful story and one filled with sadness. The sadness makes it hard to hold on to. People in even the best relationships encounter their share of drifting apart. We prefer to choose a more comforting story for ourselves and those we love. That is why the story of tidal drifts is both so familiar and so ignored. If we can bear the sadness, however, it replaces the impossible romantic hope of stopping time with the more realistic hope of renewal.

When we first spoke to our teenage children about this idea (uneasily, for we wondered if it was really something we wanted them to think about then), they immediately declared that the idea was wrong and next decided that it was just too sad (which had been our fear). The thought of ever growing apart, even temporarily, from their closest friends was unnerving to them. Particularly in adolescence, there is an intensity to friendship that makes us certain it will last a lifetime. Few friendships do, though. At a certain point in life, we begin to notice an interpersonal version of the second law of thermodynamics: entropy is always increasing. Tight bonds loosen. Carefully built systems come apart. Friends drift away. With that awareness, time itself begins to fill us with dread. It becomes linked with inevitable decline and with the severing of precious ties. We did not wish to push our children into that awareness too soon. We wanted them to enjoy to the fullest the certainty that *their* friendships would be everlasting.

The painful bewilderment we can feel when an important friendship just vanishes, seemingly for no reason at all except the passing of time, is the theme of a novel by Catherine Schine called *The Evolution of Jane*. At one point, Jane muses about her childhood best friend: "First Martha and I were one, now we were two. We had been twins, then we became strangers, now we were something or other, I couldn't put my finger on it."[3]

More than anything else, talking to our children helped us understand the desperate wish to tell stories of constant friendship and undying love, stories to protect them (and ourselves) from facing the inevitability of loss, the implacable movement toward greater entropy.

As a bumper sticker might say, "Drift happens," but we pray that it will not happen to us or to those we love. That is why the idea of drift in relationships is both so familiar and so regularly ignored.

We cannot deny the underlying melancholy embedded in our view of relationships: the moments of greatest closeness will be followed by a drift apart. Sometimes the gulf will become so wide that the relationship dies. Sometimes the ebb and flow of the tides changes the shoreline forever, obliterating what once was there. We are not drawing a naively upbeat picture of love or marriage. We are instead offering a realistic picture that creates a realistic set of expectations. A couple that understands the nature of relational drift is much more likely to be able to transform a drift apart into the tidal rhythm of ebbs and flows rather than just riding the current straight out to sea. That is the limited optimism we offer, but it can be a powerful force.

Drift in a Time of Mobility

An explicit appreciation of tidal drift is particularly important in modern American life because so much of our culture serves to blind us to it. The phrase "mobile society" may be overused, but that is what we are. It is even a source of national pride. Heroes in the legends of all cultures have always journeyed far from home in search of adventure but most, like Homer's Odysseus, travel a circular path that finally ends with the hero's return home. By contrast, the typical hero in American legends keeps moving on. The country was settled, first on the eastern seaboard and then progressively west, by individuals and families who were bravely willing to break away from the network of social connections within which most people live their lives. We remain a society in which parents and children, brothers and sisters, and close friends are extremely unlikely to live in the same town for the major portion of their lives.

The average number of geographical moves that an American makes in a lifetime is now seven. When two people drift apart emotionally, there is a good chance that they will not be around each other geographically for long enough to catch the changing tide that could restore their sense of closeness. For better or worse, we are not held together by stable social structures and shared responsibilities that, in more settled society, forced people to notice and put up with the ebbs and flows of closeness. Our lives therefore seem to provide us with powerful evidence that any estrangement is irreparable. In the past, chance events were more on the side of sustained connections. A decade ago, with great satisfaction after a break of many years, one of our fathers renewed a close friendship with an old medical school friend. The stimulus was a chance encounter between their wives, one that never would have occurred if either man had moved to a new town. Our easy mobility means that natural processes are much less likely to heal an estrangement and that a conscious effort is much more important to sustain a relationship over time.

In addition to our general mobility, over the last several decades the barriers to divorce have dropped dramatically. The social and economic costs of taking that step are much lower. The old burdens of shame and loss of social status have practically disappeared. This transformation is powerfully portrayed by essayist Vivian Gornick in "The End of the Novel of Love." She wonders why a novel about a marriage coming apart strikes her as merely sad, not tragic. She explains:

> I thought, If she *does* go off, what is she actually risking? When Emma Bovary was loosening her stays with a man other than her husband, or Anna Karenina running away from hers . . . people were indeed risking all for love. Bourgeois respectability had the power to make of these characters social pariahs. Strength would be needed to sustain exile. . . . Today, there are no penalties to pay, no world of respectability to be excommunicated from. . . . If the wife in *The Age of Grief* walks away from her marriage, she'll set up housekeeping on the other side of town with a man named Jerry instead of one named Dave, in ten minutes make a social life the equivalent of the one her first marriage had provided her, and in two years she and her new husband will find themselves at a dinner party that includes the ex-husband and his new wife: everyone chatting amiably. Two years after that, one morning in the kitchen or one night in the bedroom, she'll slip and call Jerry Dave, and they will both laugh.[4]

We will look more closely at the consequences of these changes in a later chapter (Gornick obviously but perceptively overstates the serenity of divorce). For now, we just note that although couples no longer need to endure the agonies of a marriage gone bad, they are also less likely to discover that a decrease in intimacy need not be permanent. Instead, like Jennifer and Harold, they move toward ending the marriage.

New York Times columnist Jane Brody interviewed ten long-married couples for a 1992 article on happy marriages. She found that "the thing all the couples have in common was reflected in this observation: 'Even when things were really bad, we were both too stubborn to quit.' . . . [L]ike a stockbroker who invests for the long run, the couples did not consider selling out when the price was down."[5] Today, a couple will find very little external support for that kind of stubbornness. For that matter, neither will parents and children, even though the strength of an oscillating bond can help preserve relationships that are simultaneously uncomfortable and important to us. The mother of a friend of ours has a remarkable ability to create dramatic and disruptive crises in the lives of her children (and her multiple ex-husbands). Our friend is the only relative that has not broken with her completely. Their ongoing contact provides her with a degree of stability and support, while it spares him intense feelings of guilt and loss. He can tolerate the relationship because, over time, he has developed a pattern of engagement with her punctuated by periods of withdrawal to the (relative) emotional safety of his home, his wife, and his research laboratory. The stability of his bond with his mother comes from an adult version of an infant's use of eye contact to modulate the intensity of involvement with a caregiver.

A more traditional aspect of American life also contributes to our ignorance of tidal drifts. Perhaps as a curious extension of our "pioneering spirit," Americans often equate growth with separation, with the breaking of ties. In our book *Overcoming Loneliness in Everyday Life*, we examined the origins of this equation, its fallacy, and its alarming contribution to the burden of loneliness in this country. Our local newspaper recently offered advice to parents of college freshman. The article contained reasonable statements from the coauthor of a book with an unreasonable title: *Letting Go: A Parents' Guide to Understanding the College Years*. Clearly, the author understood that the task of college students and their parents was reworking ties, not severing them, yet the title pays homage to the American myth that growth and development is about letting go.

There is a more recent but parallel myth that has emerged about marriage and divorce: an impressive number of short stories, movies, novels, and television shows proclaim that the path to personal growth regularly requires letting go of a marriage. If joy and passion are waning, then it must be time to move on. Any other choice is a retreat from "self-actualization." Yet most marriages are abandoned in a fruitless quest for romantic perfection, for Victor Hugo's changeless, "embalmed" love. What passes for personal growth is actually getting stuck in an adolescent dream world.

Growth, Guilt, and Drift

It is important to understand that the ebb and flow of closeness is not just the result of individual growth. Certainly individuals change and, we hope, grow over the course of a marriage. Certainly that growth requires complementary changes on the part of the spouse and a renegotiation of the relationship, whether it occurs explicitly or automatically. Jennifer could not possibly have gone from college student to lawyer without Harold and their marriage changing as well. The importance of permitting and nurturing change within a marriage is a commonplace wisdom in our culture of personal growth. Less well understood are the natural movements of closeness that are unrelated to changes *within* each partner. The ebb and flow that we describe is a quality of relationships, not of individuals. The problem for Jennifer was not Harold's resistance to her professional development and independence. The drift began because both of them felt so comfortable and secure about their marriage that the focus of their attention very naturally shifted for a while. In fact, Harold's support for Jennifer's pursuit of her own interests and ambitions kept him from voicing any uneasiness about her becoming somewhat more distant and unavailable. Not understanding the tidal drifts in marriages, he saw any effort to "reel her in" as selfishness. So he just watched her drift off, not sounding an alarm that she might have been grateful for. Finally, she had drifted so far from him that she was too guilty to return.

Paradoxically, while guilt about leaving can hold two people together in an unhappy marriage, it can also be one of the most powerful barriers to repairing a rift. Peter was a middle-aged writer in despair about his marriage and himself who sought psychotherapy. After ten years of marriage, he no longer felt sexually attracted to his wife but still loved her and was deeply grateful for the rich intellectual and emotional life that they shared. Their estrangement was snowballing, however, because Peter felt so guilty about his waning sexual interest that he began to withdraw from his wife in other ways. Close encounters that had previously been satisfying were now painful because they left him even more acutely aware of what was missing and his failings as a husband. An unfortunate practical consequence was that he avoided the very situations in which he might have rekindled his sexual desire. Peter's guilt, like Jennifer's, blocked the possibility of a natural, progressive reemergence of closeness.

Short- and Long-Term Cycles

Pushing the tidal metaphor just a little further lets us describe another crucial aspect of the ebb and flow in relationships. Superimposed on the twice-daily cycle of high and low tides is a slower variation in the size of each rise and fall, the twice-monthly cycle of spring and neap tides caused by the combined effects of the sun and moon. Similarly, there are shorter and longer cycles of closeness in relationships. The more rapid movements occur within an envelope of slower drifts. A diagram of this motion might look like this:

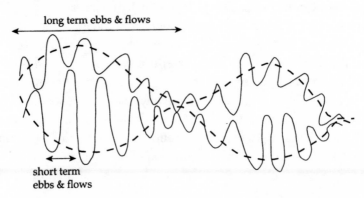

long term ebbs & flows

short term
ebbs & flows

Another way to visualize it is through the concept of fractals, patterns within patterns on an increasingly small scale. We have found that most couples experience short-term cycles of closeness and distance over periods of one or more weeks and long-term cycles lasting months to years.

Short-term cycles are often an unnoticed part of a couple's weekly routine, so built into the schedule, so automatic that they are rarely recognized as drift. Yet during the weekday bustle of work and other responsibilities, each partner's attention is regularly drawn away from the other, hopefully by genuine interest and concern for other roles that must be played and other jobs that must be done, but often just by the relentless busyness of our lives. Communication may be reduced to conveying the bare necessities of logistical information to each other. Time and energy for real dialogue, curiosity about each other's experience, or sexual relations may seem to simply disappear. A drift apart has begun. Left unchecked, it can easily begin to create feelings of estrangement.

For many couples, weekends are a time to reconnect, to spend time in real conversation, to learn a little more about each other once again, to make love in a way that claims its own time and importance. In these mundane ways, most couples reverse the drift apart before it becomes dangerous, sometimes before they even notice a change. Reconnection, however, just begins the cycle again. A renewal of closeness provides the comfort and security that each member of the couple needs to free their attention for other important interests and obligations. It is one of the ways in which a good, loving relationship contributes to a full and engaged life. A troubled relationship, by contrast, tightly captures the attention of each person, most frequently through worry or fighting. In the short run (that is, until the relationship improves or ends), it prevents a comfortable periodic drift into other concerns and leads to narrow, impoverished lives.

A periodic drift apart is not a sign of malicious neglect but an aspect of all healthy relationships. We see the same rhythm in a well-recognized stage of child development sometimes called the *rapprochement* subphase. Young toddlers venture into the world by making brief forays away from their mother, returning to the mother's lap or knee, and then going a little bit further. The child psychiatrist Margaret Mahler labeled this phenomenon "refueling." The short-term cycles of closeness that we have described are in some ways an adult version of refueling, alternately seeking comfort in a relationship and exploring the world.

Of course, these movements are not always perfectly tied to the workweek. In fact, there are signs that the cycle is lengthening, with reconnections more often occurring only every second or third week. Weekends are no longer a reliable time of refueling. Work hours are lengthening, intruding into what were once days of rest. Dual-income couples frantically jam a week's worth of domestic chores and at least a little socializing into the brief weekend interlude. The remarkable regimentation of children's out-of-school activities has led to a complementary set of demands on their parents' weekend schedules. The hallowed concept of a family-centered day of rest, contemplation, and renewal seems quaintly anachronistic to many Americans. One result is that couples who spend the workweek (in the words of a woman we interviewed) "like ships passing in the night" can easily keep right on sailing through the weekend. The rhythm of reconnection is broken or never even gets established. Regaining a sense of closeness then requires more of a self-conscious effort from one or both partners. It is no longer automatically built into the fabric of life.

We learned this lesson during a period of time when our children were young and demanding, our jobs were intense and tiring, and any attempts at "adult conversation" over dinner were reliably "jammed" by the younger generation. We began to feel as though we barely knew each other, trusting in our memories of what the other was like rather than actually knowing in an intimate way what the other was doing or experiencing. Finally, we arranged to have a teenage girl in the neighborhood babysit for just an hour and a half each Tuesday evening while we shared a nacho platter at a local pub and talked. We would find out what had happened to each other over the last week and what was on each other's mind. The ritual became so important to our marriage that, fifteen years later, we still feel a reverent joy whenever we return to that pub and a surprising devotion to their nacho platter.

In the next chapter, we will give examples of other couples who struggled to build alternate structures for reengagement and couples who stopped trying and let the long-term cycles of drift dominate their lives. In part, the short- and long-term cycles are independent of each other but not completely. The short-term effects tend to follow the contours of people's work schedules and other responsibilities, whereas the long-term effects are dominated by the slower cycles of unfolding and familiarity that we have already described in detail. Yet when the unconscious rhythms of short-term reengagement are broken for a few extra cycles, perhaps from busyness, illness, or simple complacency, the slower flow of discovery and sharing can also lose its momentum, shift direction, and begin a longer period of progressive alienation.

The long-term ebbs of intimacy present a much more direct threat to our romantic ideals. Frequently, these ebbs develop with a glacial slowness that does not produce a feeling of movement apart but instead a belated awakening to the presence of distance and estrangement. Even in that awakening, what most people feel they have discovered is an irretrievable loss of love rather than one of love's slow cycles. In their grief and turmoil, they frequently bring about an unnecessary end to the relationship, as Jennifer did. Or more subtly, there may be a silent giving up on the relationship and one or both members of the couple begins to let moments of possible reconnection go unnoticed or even actively avoid them, which was Peter's story.

Drifting Back In

Yet there are many ways of reestablishing connection, closeness, and even passion. The waning of connection itself sets in motion many forces that can turn the tides, if only they are allowed to. Surprisingly, one such force is jealousy. From Othello's diabolically misguided rage to contemporary newspaper stories about "crimes of passion," its potential for destruction has been vividly portrayed. What gets missed is its role in reversing the direction of drift. It can function both as an alarm and as a motive for efforts at reengagement. Of course, if the alarm is too sensitive, it becomes a prison to the one who is loved. If the jealousy itself is too intense, it becomes a reason for punishment instead of loving reconnection. Nevertheless, in modest doses jealousy can act as a gentle break on the natural drift toward progressive engagement with fascinating strangers or exciting new projects. At its best (though admittedly jealousy is not reliably at its best), it does not require one's partner to live a deprived and narrow life but reminds her or him that energy, time, and attention must be devoted to the relationship, to a rediscovery of the seemingly familiar person who has now been enriched by new involvements. That process of discovery in turn may recapture the original thrill of an unfolding romance and begin a movement toward being together again. Harold paid a high price for completely suppressing as mere selfishness his jealousy about Jennifer's growing interest in both her legal studies and Robert.

To make things even more complicated, our romantic ideals, which are so destructive if too rigidly held, can also contribute to a "drift alarm system" if they remind us of the blissful state that we must periodically reach for even if it can never be captured and frozen. Romantic dreams reduce our complacency about movements toward entropy in relationships, as long as their impossible perfection does not lead to catastrophic despair. The longing for meaningful conversation and the longing for sexual closeness that grow during drifts apart also act as powerful forces for reconnection, although women and men tend to differ (at least currently) in which they miss the most.

Finally, shared projects reengage us, whether they are thrown at us by fate or consciously sought as a way of revitalizing a marriage. In a study of married couples with children under five years old, we found that when the mother worked part time, the father was most likely to be drawn into child-care responsibilities. Couples who approached child care as a shared task were also most likely to have experienced an increased sense of closeness over those very stressful years. By contrast, couples in which both parents had full-time jobs or where the father worked and the mother was a full-time homemaker felt more on separate trajectories that threatened to take them further apart over time.

A major concern these days is that shared tasks and responsibilities are much less likely to automatically be part of a marriage than in eras when family farms and family businesses were more common. The demands of daily life cannot be counted on to refocus a couple's attention on the same struggle. Instead, they are often pulled apart by the demands made on each of them. The creation of shared projects that revitalize and stabilize a marriage usually requires a conscious effort, a subject we will discuss in more detail when we examine strategies for coping with tidal drift.

Phase-Shifts

The task can be daunting at times. Repeated moves apart and together can bring about lasting changes in people, wearing them down like the erosion of the coastline by the action of the tides. The movements of each individual in a couple may also be out of phase, one member seeking greater closeness just when the other is moving away, sometimes (in a situation familiar to couples therapists) daring to seek greater closeness *only* when the other is moving away. A diagram of these movements would look something like this:

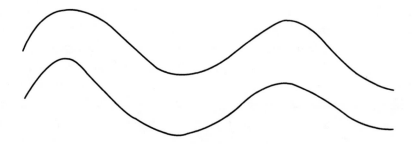

Gail and Henry Jackson were high school sweethearts whose wedding quickly followed their graduation. After their initial passion waned, they settled into a fairly common pattern: Henry was focused on creating and "growing" a retail business while Gail raised their children, looked after the home, and with increasing desperation sought more emotional intimacy and sexual involvement with Henry than he was willing to give. After a decade of uneasy stability, Gail began to think about affairs with other men and perhaps a marital separation. As she began drifting, Henry became the pursuer but his longing for greater closeness only lasted as long as she was moving away. Soon they were caught in a tide that carried them back and forth but never closer together. The pattern is a staple of romantic comedies—very easy to laugh at and very painful to live through.

The Jacksons' story also illustrates two other obstacles to sustaining a relationship over time. First, both members of a couple might not have the same comfort point for closeness or they might be more comfortable expressing closeness in different ways. Gender-based stereotypes (with a degree of truth that we shall examine later) assert that women are more comfortable with closeness than men and that men are more likely to view sex as the primary mode of experiencing closeness. Gail and Henry partly fit and partly confound those stereotypes. The second obstacle they illustrate is reflected in the phrase "after their initial passion waned." It returns us to our central concern. The waning of initial passion is a common experience. What should we make of it?

Classifying and Misclassifying Love

One of the most enduring concepts in academic writings about love is the distinction between *passionate* and *companionate* love. Most simply, it is a contrast between experiences of unsettled, often acquisitive longing and a more peaceful, generous intertwining of lives. The distinction has been a part of Western thought since the ancient Greeks distinguished between two kinds of love: *eros* and *agape*. It captures an important complexity sometimes hidden behind monolithic images of love.[6] Common wisdom teaches that passion is dominant early in a relationship and then fades, to be replaced in lasting marriages by more companionate feelings. There is an important grain of truth here, but it is too easily exaggerated.

A 1993 study assessed passionate love in couples passing through one of three life transitions: marriage, parenthood, and the empty nest.[7] Although passionate love decreased a bit with increasing length of marriage, the decline was slight. How can these findings be reconciled with the common experience of initial passion waning? The answer, of course, is through understanding the ways that passion ebbs and flows. Passion and longing are most bound up with movement *toward* the other, whereas companionate feelings are more closely related to being *with* the other. Companionate love is both magnificent in its own right and also helps sustain a connection through the ebbs and flows of passion. Another recent study found that passionate love was the best predictor of relationship satisfaction across different ethnic groups.[8] Its waning matters to most of us and happens to most of us, but it is not irreversible. Couples whose level of passion is still high as their children are leaving home have repeatedly re-created passion in their marriage. They do not preserve it "happily ever after" from their wedding night.

Yet many spouses are long gone before the children leave home. Studies of passion in lasting marriages tell only half the story. We must also look at marriages that fail. Some tides never turn and, like a riptide, carry the swimmer straight out to sea.

2

When Drift Goes Unchecked

From Cycles of Closeness to Permanent Estrangement

Relationships are always in motion. Shifting feelings of closeness are an aspect of their essential nature, not a demonstration of an individual's character flaws. Even day-to-day changes are perfectly normal. Most couples get used to ongoing motion, even if they are not fully aware of it. When two people live together, share at least some undistracted time together, talk and touch regularly, then renewals of closeness tend to happen more or less automatically.

Sometimes a different kind of motion gets started. One or both members of a couple who seem to still love each other begin to avoid or even actively thwart the moments that might lead to reconnection. Instead of cycles of closeness, they begin to experience a progressive drift further apart. This change is usually triggered by one of three situations: a sequence of ever-increasing hurt feelings within the couple; an external event that impinges powerfully on the relationship; or a shift of the exciting sense of curiosity and "unfolding" to someone new. We will examine each of these scenarios in turn, beginning with the all-too-common spiral of hurt feelings, a disaster that can start innocently enough with just one or two missed moments of reconnection in the tidal ebb and flow.

Estrangement

The concept of tidal drift is both intuitive and peculiar at the same time. Some might ask, "Well, sure there's drift but so what?" Others might comment even more skeptically, "I never noticed this drift business. What exactly do you mean?" The drift apart is often extremely gradual and, in many couples, it is regularly reversed (if only for a little while) by schedules that create some private time together on weekends. The result is that most couples either do not notice or do not care about the ever-present short-term changes in their intimacy. Even the week-to-week ebbs and flows are worth noticing, however, because they are the heartbeat of the relationship. If irregular rhythms occur and the reliable pattern of small reconnections breaks down, as often happens when one member is sick, traveling, or out of commission in some other way, the couple may find themselves *estranged* with little warning.

The word "estrangement" speaks volumes about how we feel when it happens: "He became a stranger to me." "I might as well have been living with a stranger." Do experiences like these occur only in a relationship that has gone terribly awry? We don't think so. Instead, most people find that after a physical or emotional absence, even if it is from someone they know well and love, a curious shyness and awkwardness sets in that takes time to overcome. The more temperamentally shy a person is or the longer the absence, the more this awkwardness is conscious and leads to a transient *self-consciousness*. The thoughts that accompany these moments of estrangement might sound like this: "Am I really tied to this person for life when I hardly know him/her at all? How did this ever happen? What is wrong with me that I feel this way?" It helps to know that these worrisome feelings are present at times in all good relationships. The only cure for this "rustiness" is to understand it and allow private time together to gradually reverse the trend. These "little estrangements" are something that most people prefer to keep to themselves instead of confess to their partner, because they feel it is probably their own peculiarity rather than a shared experience. Only if these feelings persist for weeks and months despite time alone together and repeated attempts to reach out do couples start to talk openly about feeling estranged.

We can recognize more easily a closely related state of estrangement in a college student who returns home to find himself ill at ease around his family, as if he didn't really belong anymore. Reassurance may be offered by an older person who understands that the feeling is typical for someone who has been away from home for nine months. The student, however, is not reassured until he has spent enough time around family to feel comfortable again. Before that happens, he may even suspect that a permanent rift has developed between him and his family. But even wise adults who offer reassurance to returning college students are surprised and worried if a similar phenomenon occurs with a spouse after a trip or a period of sexual abstinence.

The state of mild estrangement that follows a short separation or a lack of physical closeness for a couple of weeks is part of the normal ebb and flow of intimacy and should be treated accordingly. It must be seen as a normal event in any loving relationship, unremarkable and certainly not a sign of terrible problems, but requiring attention and time to overcome. Without this recognition, a cycle of estrangement and hurt feelings may begin in which each partner inadvertently exacerbates the rift, all the while thinking that it is the other person's fault.

A salesman named Joe Kamal, whose job required him to travel for several days each week, had a typical experience of mild estrangement getting out of control. His family had become accustomed to his frequent absences, but his wife Anne resented her role as a "single mother" during many weekdays. Gradually, her anger took the form of ignoring her husband's return home. As she said, "It disrupts the family routine, and anyway, we don't want to have to make a fuss about Joe as if he were a child, when this happens every week." For his part, Joe would come home hoping to be welcomed like a heroic hunter who had killed a wild boar for his family. When his wife and children (taking Anne's cue) would go about their business without paying attention to him, he felt neglected and unappreciated.

Soon Joe stopped planning weekend nights out with Anne to pay her back for the lack of special welcome when he returned from his trips. Anne felt that he was acting distant for no apparent reason and decided that she had better get used to having fun without him. She began arranging to spend weekend nights "out with the girls" because she was too "sick of being cooped up all week" to sit around the house on the weekend. Joe was then indignant. He could not believe that Anne would squander their "date nights" on her girlfriends. Finally their vicious cycle of hurt feelings became so intense that Anne announced to Joe that the marriage was in serious trouble and he would have to come to couples' therapy. Achieving this level of misunderstanding often takes much longer, but Joe and Anne's situation demonstrates how easily small slights can build into large estrangements.

Sounding the Alarm

An understanding of drift leads to a corresponding appreciation of just how important it is to build regular opportunities for reconnection into a marriage. A shared attention to breaks in the restorative rhythm is the best way to keep ordinary experiences of distance from spiraling into a major crisis. Each feeling wounded by the other, Joe and Anne did just the opposite. They began to dismantle the opportunities for restoring connection that were still present in their life together until Anne finally sounded an alarm.

Although shared attention to restoring closeness might be ideal, it is much more common for just one person to notice the drift apart and become alarmed, often to the surprise of the partner. Just as there are clear differences (both personal and cultural) in how close we stand to another person when we talk, there are clear differences in how far we can drift from someone we love before we start to feel uneasy. To repeat an earlier image, our "distance alarms" vary in how sensitive they are. Often the spouse who remains comfortable and has not yet noticed the drift will try to convince the one who has that she is oversensitive, imagining things, and perhaps in need of psychotherapy or medication. (In a culture like ours, which expects women to be the keepers of relationships, a woman is likely to notice the distance first.) It takes strength of character to be able to stand by one's awareness of a slow-moving, murky phenomenon and not just agree that it is one's own neurotic problem. If the "distance-noticing" partner can stick to her guns, however, and persuade her spouse that there is a danger to be taken seriously, the couple must then understand that they need to allocate sufficient time to be alone together to straighten things out. It is also important for the partner who has noticed the increasing distance not to talk about the rift in words or tones that are so blaming or panicky that she drives her spouse even further away.

Joan and Bill Frankel

Joan Frankel was an intense forty-six-year-old college administrator who was brought up in rural South Dakota where even the women acted "macho." She explained that when she and family members drove across the state together, they usually sat in silence. Idle chatter was frowned upon, even if there were only two people in the car. She felt that she was not one to express neediness until she was desperate. Her husband, a gregarious Jewish entrepreneur, would become gripped by new projects, often working deep into the night, which left his wife feeling ignored and neglected. The couple had no children.

Even with her early childhood training in how to act "macho," Joan found herself feeling so unhappy and lonely that she brought her husband into couples' therapy. Bill suggested to the therapist that Joan was "clinically depressed" and needed Prozac. It did not occur to him that, in an indirect way, his wife might have been trying to signal that she was feeling distant and cut off from him. In frustration, Joan began their treatment by announcing to Bill that she felt suicidal. As the initial sessions unfolded, her aversion to expressing need became clear to both of them, along with her sensitivity to any increasing distance between them. He, on the other hand, had few "distance sensors." He declared with conviction that he always felt close to her—even when he was working late nights and weekends. He saw his love for her as the source of both his creativity and contentment but, he said, unless she spelled things out for him, he wouldn't remember to give their relationship any attention because his work consumed him during these creative periods.

The solution that worked best for them was to dedicate one day each weekend to shared time, whether either Bill or Joan expressed a need for it or not. Reconnection no longer required either person to seem weak by begging for time together. The regularity of it kept them from losing track of each other under the pressure of their hectic schedules. If they had been religious, they might have counted on the sabbath ritual of a day of rest to hold work at bay, but since they were not, they had to agree to it in couples' therapy. In addition, Bill was supposed to practice drawing his wife out when she looked or sounded distressed, whereas Joan promised to experiment with expressing her needs more clearly. With a couples' therapist to remind them of their tasks, they began to feel close again and Joan emerged from her depression.

Clearly, we would hope that if one member of a couple has a more sensitive distance alarm than her partner, she would mention her discomfort long before it reached the point of suicidal feelings. Joan's inhibition, derived from the cowboy culture of South Dakota, is just an exaggeration of what most people feel if they see themselves "whining" about loneliness in a relationship. Men are brought up to never make a fuss, no matter how "out in the cold" they might feel. Women have been allowed to make more of a fuss, but it was considered a confirmation of their weakness, rather than an essential function. Naturally, women as well as men now choose to avoid a devalued role and fear acting too whiny or babyish. It is not easy to be the one who regularly complains about the increasing distance and the need for shared time and attention.

In the best of worlds, both members of a couple would jointly bear responsibility for noticing and responding to a drift apart, rather than making one partner appear pathetic and needy and the other strong and self-sufficient. But the still too-rigid gender roles in our culture have not laid the groundwork for women and men to guard equally against the danger of mutual alienation. Women much more often are allowed and expected to be the watchdogs of the relationship, as Joan ultimately was, even with her South Dakota toughness. Men have responded to this division of labor by dreading a wife's need to talk things out, assuming that the talk will be about their neglect and incompetence in the relationship. Only by recognizing ebb and flow as a constant process that requires an alarm function to be present *somewhere* in a couple can we get men and women to work together to preserve passionate relationships through repeated acts of reconnection.

Ignoring the Alarm

An alarm is of no value if no one knows what to do when it goes off. At times, both members of a couple may sense a growing estrangement and have no idea how to respond to it. One couple we know had difficulties with the "overfertility" of the wife. Lianne Teneda had a demanding one-year-old child who required all of her energy. Despite the assiduous use of birth control, she became pregnant again. Neither she nor her husband Mark felt ready to deal with a second child, so Lianne had an abortion. This event was much more troubling to both of them than they would have predicted. Lianne dealt with her sorrow by extraordinary caretaking and closeness with her toddler. Mark felt terrified that if they resumed a normal sex life, she would again get pregnant accidentally and perhaps become seriously depressed, a danger that had been foreshadowed by her response to the abortion. So he devoted himself fanatically to his hobbies of writing and gardening, hoping to dampen both his sexual interest and the hurt feelings that arose from finding himself so left out of his wife and child's couplehood.

Three years later, when Lianne started feeling energetic and liberated because her child had started kindergarten, she felt a growing rage at Mark, who had seemed to manage so well without her sexually. It never occurred to her that he was trying to protect her, at great cost to himself, from having to choose between another abortion or being overburdened prematurely by a second child. Instead, she felt spurned by his devotion to his hobbies. Mark felt like an intruder between his daughter and wife. His sacrifice of sexual satisfaction for his wife's sake had backfired terribly because Lianne couldn't understand how he could love her and yet do without her for three years. Meanwhile, there had been such a long period of abstinence that she couldn't remember how it had ever felt to be attracted to her husband. Couples' therapy was unable to reverse their estrangement. Each felt much too painfully hurt by what each of them felt was the other's long rejection. The couple made plans to separate.

In this case, once again, the tendency for both partners to play their cards close to the vest resulted in catastrophe. As they both felt more and more wounded, they nursed their hurt in solitude and kept up with the ordinary forms of life, so their spouse hardly detected any true feelings or intentions. Mark thought he was doing his wife a favor by not imposing on her sexually. Lianne felt spurned but threw herself into child care with such enthusiasm that her husband never detected her hurt. Each thought they were on a one-way street with no choice about what must be done. Each tried to be a good sport. They both suppressed their inner anxieties, ignoring a growing sense of alarm at the distance between them. But the good sportsmanship gradually wore thin, and the years of concealed hurt feelings led to a tragic misinterpretation of each other's signals and finally to permanent estrangement.

Effects of Physical or Emotional Illness

Couples often deal intuitively with the short-term ebbs and flows over many years, only to be undone when one person is touched by serious physical or emotional illness. Many forms of illness, from pneumonia to depression, cause a decrease in energy level and a related increase in irritability. The sick individual may lose his or her usual flexibility. This change can catch a partner off guard, particularly one who is also depleted by caretaking, extra responsibilities, and worry. Soon the well spouse may lose sight of the months or years of reasonable flexibility that preceded the current troublesome state. Psychiatrist and author Peter Kramer addresses the issue of a depressed spouse in his book, *Should You Leave?*[1] He suggests that if one member of a couple starts to act mysteriously difficult, depression should always be a considered as a cause. We would add that occasionally feelings of insecurity or inferiority make a person much less able to express need or hurt. Keeping feelings to oneself for too long can be physiologically stressful and may contribute to an emerging depression. No matter how you trace the etiology of depression, however, there is no doubt that depressed people are difficult to be around and less likely to be able to roll with the tides than nondepressed people. One sad consequence is that they often push away those whose love and comfort might be restorative.

Similarly, even minor physical illnesses can cause rifts to develop, especially when people expect themselves to carry on as usual with jobs and domestic chores despite the exhaustion brought on by illness. For example, a man with a cold, a mild flu, or minor pain might go on with life as usual, refusing to change a demanding schedule and doing his best not to complain. "That's just what men do," he might say to himself. Yet his increased exhaustion soon leads to an increased irritability and self-centeredness, not an unusual result of sickness. His partner notices only the self-centered hostility and feels pushed away, without understanding the cause. Highly achievement-oriented adults, both women and men, are particularly at risk because they abhor any sign of passivity in themselves and, rather than give in to the wish to be taken care of when sick, frequently take out their dissatisfaction with themselves on their nearest and dearest. Pretty soon they are feeling both unproductive and unloved. The extra kindness of the healthy partner may soon be withdrawn in the face of resentment and ingratitude. Relatively few people know intuitively how to be gracious patients who recognize the temporary neediness stemming from their illness, acknowledge it, and express gratitude for the extra help that they actually want.

A more alarming rift began for another couple when medical problems during the birth of their first child left the wife with intermittent weakness and pain for almost six months. New fathers commonly feel pushed aside by the intense bond between mother and infant (more on this in a subsequent chapter). These difficult but ordinary feelings were drastically heightened because, in her weakened state, the mother devoted almost all of her limited energy and attention to the baby. Her husband tried to be understanding, but as the months stretched on, he began to feel unloved and irrelevant at home. He feared that he had been used by his wife to get a child and was now discarded. Despite his love for both his wife and his new son, he began to focus most of his energy on his job. As the spiral of hurt feelings continued, they began couples' therapy with the wife sadly explaining that her husband had stopped loving her.

Almost any event that causes a member of the couple to want to avoid physical contact for a while is potentially dangerous. Recent research suggests that physical contact increases levels of endorphins and oxytocin, neurochemicals that induce feelings of well-being and may even be involved in the creation of affectionate bonds.[2] Childbearing, menopause, injuries, medications that lead to decreased sexual drive, all these can take their toll on the regular physical closeness that is so important to sustaining a loving relationship.

Indignation can also be an obstacle to the restorative effects of touch and sexual contact; for example, the not uncommon indignation of a woman who feels she is only appreciated as a "sex object" or a man who feels chronically rejected. Evie Warren came from a big family and had always imagined herself the mother of at least several children. After the birth of a first child, she and her husband Tim both wanted to have more children, but he also wanted to develop a sensual relationship with his wife in which they experimented more with sexual play and took pleasure in regular touching. Evie was a bit skeptical that this adventure could ever happen. Her cultural upbringing had taught that you were absolutely not supposed to think sexual thoughts or explore any sexual pleasure except for the express purpose of procreation. She felt that, over the years, she had tried hard to "become more sexual and sensual" but it had not worked. As far as she was concerned, sex was certainly not the most important thing in the marriage. Tim argued that she did not just relegate sex to a secondary status but that she now wanted to keep it out of the marriage altogether. He felt chronically rejected by her lack of enthusiasm.

When Evie got pregnant a second time, it turned out to be an ectopic pregnancy that threatened her life. She was so spooked that she felt they would have to avoid sex for years. Even though she tried to put the pain and danger of that pregnancy out of her mind, she could not forget it. It colored her attitude to all of Tim's overtures. Tim stopped making as many sexual overtures as he had in the past because he too had been terrified by his wife's brush with death. Although they did not seriously contemplate divorce, their relationship became marked by bitterness, bickering, and tension. Their physical estrangement turned into an emotional one. Any attempt at reconnection was blocked by the combination of shared fears and shared hurts, so neither touch nor words offered a path back to each other.

Effects of New Interests

Not only tragedy generates riptides. Even something as simple and desirable as a person discovering a new interest or starting a new project can disrupt the rhythm of reconnections that had previously worked for a couple. The crucial question then becomes how each person responds to the new current, with its dual possibilities of renewal and danger. One couple was catapulted into trouble when the husband, who had always been interested in photography, discovered computer software that let him doctor his pictures. Justin Kornbluth was equally fascinated by the techniques and the results, which seemed magical to him. He often lost track of time when he was immersed in his new projects. Meanwhile, his wife Carol, who felt left out and suspected that he was deliberately pushing her away, concluded that he was "afraid of intimacy." Justin kept insisting he was only enjoying a hobby he'd always loved and in fact the reason he felt free to pursue it again was precisely because he was happy and secure in his marriage. He begged his wife not to take it personally and promised to limit his time at the computer so she wouldn't feel abandoned every evening. Carol tried not to take it personally, but her "distance alarm" was sounding too loudly. Justin really was a little oblivious to the importance of shared activities to sustain their connection instead of just happily assuming that the connection was unchangingly secure. There really was a danger that they would just drift apart. Unfortunately, rather than talking about how hurt she felt by the change in him, she hurt him in turn. She began to complain that he had "gone off the deep end." Picking up a theme from the daily papers, she labeled him a computer addict. He then started avoiding her because her portrayal of him was just too unsettling. "Maybe there is something really wrong with me for enjoying this so much," he wondered. His wife proposed couples' therapy to improve their communication.

In therapy, Justin came to appreciate both how hurt Carol felt and the genuine risks to a marriage he cherished if he continued to take their feelings of closeness for granted. She in turn understood that her response to feeling pushed away by her husband was to pay him back in kind—and it was working all too well. She also was able to see a connection to her childhood, when her father always brought work home from the office and she felt that she could never "win" over his work no matter how hard she tried to divert him. Carol was extremely sensitive to feeling ignored and deeply pessimistic about her ability to do anything about it. She came to see that a temporary ebb in Justin's attention was not automatically a catastrophe, whereas he began to recognize the importance of keeping it temporary.

Sometimes a lucky couple goes along in a richly fulfilled life, with satisfying work, enjoyable hobbies, and time for family, friends, and coworkers, but they simply forget to nourish their relationship with each other, which needs enough relaxed private time for conversation and for touching. It's a little like a large landowner who takes very good care of his far-flung acreage but forgets to water the home vegetable garden because it has always flourished. Sometimes one member of a couple loves to socialize with others so much that he or she forgets that a couple can grow apart if they are always surrounded by others and just a little more "on" than they would be in moments alone together. The effort to be interesting, charming, or compassionate almost always get directed to a fresh audience rather than toward one's partner. If a spouse who prefers more private time together goes along with the social whirl, trying to be a good sport, the couple may start to feel estranged. As time alone for sexual and conversational contact diminishes, the rustiness and shyness mentioned earlier may begin to develop, even though it might look to the outside world as though the couple is inseparable. Though inseparable, they may find themselves feeling so awkward when alone with each other that they start to need the constant presence of others to avoid facing their estrangement.

The Threat of the Frank Conversation

Our brief review of situations that create destructive cycles of hurt feelings would seem to suggest a simple antidote: frank private discussions in which feelings of rejection are acknowledged and the reasons for each others' actions and responses are mutually understood. Since the hurt feelings are so often the result of misunderstandings, it should not be hard for a couple to get back on track and, with the air cleared, begin to spend enough time together to restart the slow movement toward renewed closeness. Clearly, there are major obstacles to this seemingly simple solution. In the privacy of our consulting rooms, we see in couple after couple that the necessary conversations have been avoided by one or another partner. Most often (recognizing both the risks and value of generalizations based on gender), the woman has been trying to get her husband to talk things over and he has avoided these discussions like the plague. Why would a man want to escape an encounter that could set him back on the road to emotional closeness and warmth?

Part of the answer is that he simply doesn't believe it will work. The vicious cycle of hurt feelings is powerfully demoralizing. Caught in its grip, we lose faith in our ability to do or say anything that doesn't end up making things worse. This pessimism is frequently compounded by a man's sense that he is outmatched by his wife in any discussion about feelings or relationships. Many couples that end up in couples' therapy encounter another obstacle. The wife has been using guilt provocation as her main method of "reeling her husband in," and it is absolutely *not* working. An unfortunate (and we hope transitional) side effect of feminism's empowerment of women is that, in sisterly appreciation of women's plight over the centuries, some women adopt a shrill "why have you done this to me when I am already so martyred" tone that their husbands come to dread. We suspect that today's women, who have taken so much more on their plate, trying to be mothers, wives, homemakers, and career women, are left with chronic guilt over not doing as much for their families as their own mothers did. The guilt carries with it so much anxiety over what it means to be "doing your share" that it is a blessed relief to be able to take time off from self-blame to blame someone else instead. Usually it is the husband who takes the brunt of it, and he soon learns that "a talk about how the relationship is doing" is always a losing proposition.

Not that husbands don't have their own standard guilt-provoking moves. Paradoxically, a man who is drawn into more active roles in housekeeping and child care is more likely to become hypercritical of his wife's activity on the home front. Our informal impression is that, with a closer view of housekeeping tasks, these men are acutely aware of a certain slipping down from the high standards of their own mothers, who were often full-time homemakers. Although these stereotypes don't do justice to individual complexity, they describe a type of marital interaction that is actually quite prevalent nowadays and may reflect living in a transitional culture that is still getting used to the consequences of most women working outside the home. Changing roles within a marriage always opens up new areas for blame, guilt, and hurt feelings.

A second obvious antidote to the cycle of hurt feelings is to spend more time alone together, standard advice from couples' therapists and marriage columns that is incompletely understood even by many of those offering the advice. When a therapist suggests time alone together, many couples immediately start to plan a vacation or at least a long weekend away together. A vacation alone is anything but hum-

drum and it does help overcome the shyness that accompanies estrangement. The shared relaxation it provides can often jump-start the couple
on the road back to intimacy. The simple declaration that both partners
care enough to go to the trouble of planning something special together
can also help. But the real solution that the couple must search for is
how to establish regular periods of intimacy in their everyday life, without a stressless schedule and a romantic setting to help them relax. They
must acquire the habit of taking time for each other even though the
usual thousand tasks are pressing in upon them, demanding to be done.
They must build a cycle of reconnections into the flow of ordinary life.

Finally, we must stress the importance of common projects and interests if a couple is to have a decent chance of creating reliable patterns of
reconnection and closeness. During the early years of parenting, when
children need so much attention and thought, husbands and wives often
cannot help connecting with each other around the tasks that have to be
done. One problem with too-efficient schedules is that the wife and husband may become very separate in their child-care responsibilities and
feel like two shiftworkers on different shifts who don't have any time together. Even then, much discussion is likely to take place if only to work
out logistics. Studies we have done in the past suggest that parents often
feel very close during their children's early years. When the children
grow up and out, however, raising children disappears as a shared enterprise and, if no other joint projects replace it, soon the parents' lives may
be so separate that they lose contact with each other. The "empty nest"
moment is a time when a couple may have to "engineer" new shared projects into a marriage so that they have the sensation of a new chapter
opening in their lives *together*, providing once again the rush of unfolding
excitement that they remember from first love.

Recognizing the Normality of Ebb and Flow

So far, we have described the ebbs and flows of closeness that form the
life pulse of every good relationship. The rhythm arises from the nature
of closeness, an experience of moving toward someone, not a static condition. A couple must reconnect intimately through touching and conversation every few days or at least weeks in order to continue to feel

close. When this rhythm is lost, the relationship starts to feel empty and estranged to one or both people, a warning signal that a "relationship danger" is developing. Couples need to work together to recover from this commonplace consequence of being comfortably secure with each other and "letting the relationship go" for too long. Perhaps they had taken for granted that the relationship would take care of itself because their love was so strong. Or it may be that some external event, such as sickness or absence, affected their ebb and flow rhythm in an unanticipated way. These are all ordinary moments in any lasting relationship, yet we have seen how easy it is to slip into a vicious cycle of hurt feelings and escalating estrangement when they occur. A heightened awareness of the very ordinariness of ebb and flow can help a couple to avoid the unnecessary feelings of rejection that so frequently come along with the ebbs. The answer is not, however, to replace panic with complacency. There must also be enough recognition of the potential damage that follows a break in the rhythm to prompt a couple to repair the rift.

For two people to take good care of a passionate relationship, therefore, at least one of them must be able hear the alarm bell ringing and say something about it in a way that is not so condemning of the other person that he or she stops listening. Then there needs to be enough talk so that each person is not nursing old hurts close to his or her breast, playing at being more martyred than the other. This talk takes time, which must be wrenched away from all the other competing demands that offer convenient excuses for side-stepping the whole question. Finally, when enough talk has been shared, there also needs to be enough touching so the couple can overcome their physical estrangement. Only then can the flow of closeness be reestablished and the old rhythm begin once more. But not all feelings of rejection are misunderstandings, which leads us to the subject of infidelity, temptation, and fascinating strangers.

3

Whirlpools of Temptation
and Jealousy

"But King Solomon loved many strange women"
1 Kings 11.1

Some years ago, a psychiatric resident (a physician receiving specialty training in psychiatry) sat down to discuss a patient she had just seen for the first time. "I need some help," said this usually self-assured young woman. She looked like she couldn't decide whether to laugh or scream. "The patient is here because he can't keep an erection with any woman other than his wife."

The story serves us well as teachers. It swiftly carries almost any seminar into a lively examination of the place of moral judgments in psychiatry. The responses we encounter also highlight the tension that exists in our society and within many individuals about the "naturalness" of roving desire. The tension is an ancient one. After all, Solomon is renowned for his wisdom and even he succumbs to the allure of exotic strangers (and, through these strange women, to the temptation of strange gods). The Bible's stern and explicit condemnation cannot completely erase a more complicated message embedded in the story for those who wish to hear it and then whisper to themselves, "If even Solomon . . ." The resident's patient is a perfect, if unconscious, embodiment of our warring views about marital fidelity.

The Bible does not condemn Solomon for marital infidelity (consider that "he had seven hundred wives ... and three hundred concubines") but for his religious infidelity to a jealous God. Yet there is a profound narrative wisdom in linking a lust for strange women with a lust for strange gods. It underscores two aspects of human nature that are crucial to an understanding of infidelity: the desire for novelty and the way in which sharing in one realm leads to sharing in others (in the story of Solomon, from sharing sexual passion to sharing religious rites; in a more common story nowadays, from sharing a work project to sharing a bed).

Novelty

To speak briefly in the stark language of behaviorism, "Repeated exposure to a very positive stimulus leads to an increasingly negative emotional response to it. . . . Complex organisms have a need for variety or novelty; change of stimulus conditions can thus be reinforcing."[1] Put more simply, we get bored with even the best things in our lives and can be reawakened by something new. Put perhaps simple-mindedly, it's our family's tomato argument: traveling together years ago, we debated whether or not we could possibly lose our joy in the taste of freshly picked tomatoes if we had them too often. The official answer from experimental psychology is yes. Sameness dulls the senses and erodes our pleasure. These are not surprising assertions. Of course they must apply to love and sex and marriage. Of course our experiences of intimacy and passion, when readily available, are bound to wane in intensity over time, just like our response to any other stimulus.

With lasting power, Gustave Flaubert's famous nineteenth-century novel *Madame Bovary* portrays a woman destroyed by the intolerable gulf between her commonplace marriage and her romantic ideal, "that marvelous passion which, until then, had been like a great rosy-plumaged bird soaring in the splendors of poetic skies."[2] She thinks she captures it in the initial excitement of courtship, but as the intensity wanes, "she could not bring herself to believe that the calm in which she was living was the happiness she dreamed of."[3] She tries to re-create romantic intensity in her marriage by "following the theories in which she believed."[4] When these efforts fail, Flaubert evokes the profound joylessness of unchanging love rituals and unchanging landscapes:

> She easily convinced herself that there was no longer anything extraordinary about Charles's love for her. His raptures settled into a regular schedule; he embraced her only at certain hours. It was one habit among many, like a dessert known in advance, after a monotonous dinner.
>
> She would walk to the beech grove at Banneville, near the abandoned pavilion which stands at the corner of the wall facing the fields. . . . She would begin by looking around to see if anything had changed since her last visit. She always found everything in the same place: the foxgloves and the gillyflowers, the clumps of nettles around the stones and the patches of lichen along the three windows, whose shutters, always closed, were rotting away from their rusty iron bars. . . . Then her mind would gradually focus; sitting on the grass and poking at it with the tip of her parasol, she would ask herself over and over, "Oh, why did I ever get married?"[5]

The question intrudes into many marriages during the inevitable ebb of excitement when the rush of first passions (or in Emma Bovary's case, the illusion of first passions) subsides. It intrudes with even greater force for individuals who take any ebb in closeness as proof that love was an illusion or is inexorably dying. In these moments, the idea of recapturing novelty and intensity and the freshness of loving (or simply having sex) with somebody new can often seem to be the only hope for once again soaring with that great rosy-plumaged bird. Of course, many married men and many married women, like Emma Bovary, have affairs. In fact, some recent surveys report that most married American men *and* women have had affairs.[6] Although exact numbers are debatable, the ordinariness of extramarital sex seems well established. Our fascination with it is equally clear, in the novels and short stories of our time, on the covers of magazines and headlines of newspapers, in the gossip that excites us, in the constant flow of country songs about "cheatin'." Almost everyone in love has at one time or another wondered, "Is he (she) cheating on me?" Almost everyone in love has at one time or another wondered, "Will I cheat on him (her)?"

The ordinariness of adultery is also well established cross-culturally. The anthropologist Helen Fisher writes:

> I recently read forty-two ethnographies about different peoples past and present and found that adultery occurred in every one. Some of these peoples lived in tenements; others in row houses or thatched huts. Some raised rice; some raised money. Some were rich, some poor. Some espoused Christianity; others worshiped gods embodied in the sun, the wind, the rocks, and trees. Regardless of their traditions of marriage, despite their customs of divorce, irrespective of any of their cultural mores about sex, they all exhibited adulterous behavior—even where adultery was punished with death. . . . There exists no culture in which adultery is unknown, no cultural device or code that extinguishes philandering.[7]

Fisher sees the workings of Darwinian evolution in these powerful observations. Evolutionary psychology is currently the most fashionable scholarly discourse to enlist in defense of the naturalness of male sexual adventurism. It takes the venerated folk wisdom that "it's just men's nature" (a view that has been advanced with equal fervor by both free-love advocates and old-fashioned moralists) one step further, reasoning that the workings of evolution *require* it to be men's nature. The man who spreads his seed widely has a clear evolutionary advantage over the homebody; he will have children everywhere. Evolutionary psychologists generally assumed that women, who must carry the child rather than just spread the seed, were better served by monogamy as an evolutionary strategy—hence the battle of the sexes. Fisher (along with anthropologist Sarah Hrdy) challenges that prevailing belief with a more egalitarian view. She sees Darwinian advantages for women as well as men in having multiple sexual partners. Although multiple partners will not lead women to have more children, it may let them provide their offspring with more resources and more protection in an insecure world.

Whether these arguments are correct and our evolutionary past has left us "hardwired" to cheat, infidelity is a common occurrence, long understood to be a part of many men's lives and, increasingly, women's lives. (It remains unclear just how much of the reported increase in adultery among married women represents an actual change in sexual behavior or merely a change in the willingness to report sexual behavior.) It is also clear that the lure of novelty and freshness and the sense of discovery (and sometimes conquest) of a new lover play a crucial role in the experience that leads to infidelity.

Yet the picture we have presented is clearly incomplete. A quest for novelty is not the only driving force in most people's lives, not even their sexual lives. Predictability may not sound "sexy," but it is a powerful and basic desire. Much of mankind's energy throughout history has been devoted to creating more predictability in a dangerously unpredictable world. That enterprise may be most obvious in our approach to the natural world, but it is just as important in our dealings with each other. Social customs and roles transform an encounter with a frighteningly unpredictable and potentially dangerous stranger into a comfortable and safe exchange. The near-universal custom of marriage is an effort to provide a measure of safe predictability in our sexual lives and in the lives of our children. To know a spouse well means to know something about what he or she is likely to do and how he or she is likely to feel. The profound considerateness of love and the precious sense of being well-cared for cannot exist without that kind of knowing. The celebrated comforts of home and hearth depend on confident advance knowledge of what we will find there. In the cozy shelter of that reassuring predictability, we may sometimes enjoy being surprised a bit, but not too much.

Wanting It All

So most of us want it all—adventure and comfort, freedom and commitment, the novel and the familiar. The psychologist Leslie Baxter (among many others) suggests that human relationships can best be understood by examining the "dialectics" in them, meaning the ongoing tension and struggle between two contradictory but interdependent tendencies. He cites three basic contradictions in personal relationships: autonomy-connection, openness-closedness, and novelty-predictability.[8] His theory of dialectics fits very well with our description of ebb and flow in general. The tension between deeply held but contradictory desires, neither of which can ever be given up for good, begins to conjure up pictures of partners linked together in endlessly oscillating movement, reminiscent of the illustrations in old physics textbooks that show two masses attached by a spring in "simple harmonic motion." An affair can be a powerful reassertion of autonomy in a marriage that has begun to feel like an all-encompassing connection; it can be a daring reach for novelty in a relationship that has become too comfortably predictable. In other words, it can sometimes be an individual's attempt to regain the right balance in a relational dialectic rather than a decision to end the relationship. It certainly is a dangerous move, though, and one that frequently ends in disaster.

An obvious problem with an affair as a source of novelty is what one might call either the asymmetry of surprise in the situation or simply its unfairness. One spouse chooses to create pleasurable novelty in life; the other spouse is on the receiving end of a very unpleasant surprise in just the arena where marriage is supposed to provide predictability. They certainly don't end up with an equally satisfying balance of adventure and stability in their sex lives. Even if the problem of fairness can be solved, at least theoretically, by both spouses agreeing that each will have an affair, simple equality of extramarital sex is not a reliable solution: it only works if both spouses want the same mix of novelty and predictability in their sex lives. Often they don't. The traditional claim that men crave variety in sexual matters more than women is looking increasingly shaky. Between the era of Madame Bovary and today's covers of Cosmopolitan, many woman have become much more comfortable noticing and acknowledging an interest in sexual novelty. Still, the problem of a mismatch between two individuals married to each other is not resolved by invoking the average desires of men and women. The strategy of equal numbers of lovers for both spouses also assumes that jealousy disappears just because an arrangement is fair. Despite the sunny optimism of a phrase like "open marriage," real-life experiences are usually a lot messier.

Christopher Daggett is a more cautious example of a man who sought psychotherapy because he wanted to have sex with women other than his wife. He was a middle-aged businessman, deacon of his church, a sober and responsible member of his community, a faithful husband over thirty years who spoke wistfully of never having had even a single sexual encounter with any other woman. He felt that he did not want to pass into old age without having experienced both variety and adventure in his sexual life. He was convinced that his wife would not approve of these longings, certainly not in regard to other women, but not even as something to strive for in their relationship. He believed that his longings were natural, wanted to seize the moment, but felt so guilty that he could not proceed. He hoped that psychotherapy could relieve him of his guilt and free him to enter a life of sensual delight without having to end his marriage to a woman he respected and cherished and without having to give up his view of himself as a moral man.

The solution was obviously to find a doctor who would understand his guilt as a "neurotic problem" with roots in his past and then cure him of it. Christopher was distressed to discover that he had instead stumbled upon a psychiatrist who spoke to him of a conflict between two deeply held desires, and neither desire could be trivialized and made to disappear by labeling it an illness. His wish to be both a loyal husband and a sexual adventurer is by no means unusual; he stands out only because of his almost innocent hope that a psychiatrist could eliminate all the tension he felt between those wishes. Some version of that tension ebbs and flows in intensity over the course of almost all marriages. The efforts of couples over the ages to cope with that fluctuating tension have provided more than enough examples of adultery to prove sexual promiscuity is natural, but they have also provided more than enough examples of fidelity to prove that monogamy is natural. What is actually natural is the inescapable presence in our lives of conflicting desires.

Some would argue that this particular conflict is an absurd artifact of twentieth-century American culture. Perhaps Christopher was just unlucky to be a respectable middle-aged man in a town and a time that frowned on respectable middle-aged men taking mistresses. Consider the famous contrast between Bill Clinton's impeachment and the placid acceptance in France of former president Francois Mitterand's wife and mistress standing together at his funeral. The contrast is famous precisely because it was invoked so frequently as proof that Americans are foolishly naive about sex. Even the Bible provides a model of marriage that would get Christopher out of his bind. If only he could follow the polygamous example of Solomon and the patriarchs. As we were writing this chapter, an article appeared in the *New York Times Magazine* on "The Persistence of Polygamy" among Mormon fundamentalists in Utah. Inevitably, the religious defence of polygamy based on sacred Mormon texts is now interwoven with references to the work of evolutionary psychologists:

> "You look at the nature of men, and most of them are polygamous," says Mary Potter, who was once one of three wives of a policeman in a Salt Lake City suburb. . . . "In polygamy, men are properly channeled."
>   She and other supporters of polygamy point to recent studies that men are evolutionally [sic] wired for multiple sexual partners.[9]

Have we discovered yet another way in which we have been misled by the romantic myth, picturing eternal bliss married to our *one* true love and colliding with our fundamental nature? Or more narrowly, have we been foolish to weave the romantic myth into our vision of marriage? Other societies have understood that stable marriage can exist to serve social functions that have nothing to do with our longings for romance and have not asked the same individual to satisfy both needs. Why not follow their ancient wisdom and spare the American marriage its lovely but back-breaking burden of trying to satisfy an impossibly wide range of both spouses' needs and desires? Why not let Christopher off the hook as he hoped we would, if not through psychotherapy then through social change?

There are several well-entrenched battles hidden behind these questions, but above all there is the problem of Christopher's wife. She appears not to share her husband's vision of an ideal marriage. From Christopher's description, she is far from a feminist, but he has no doubt that she would agree with feminist critiques of marriages that let husbands have their cake and eat it too while wives remain content in the kitchen. Evolutionary arguments can never completely eliminate questions about the kind of marriage that we want to have simply by reducing all our wants to evolutionary imperatives. Freud's famous dictum *biology is destiny* has been given new life by evolutionary psychology, but it is more accurate to say that biology *shapes* our destiny. So do cultural constructs like fairness and conscience and what it means to us when acting on our desires would hurt someone we love. Furthermore, attachment behavior and bonding is clearly as much a part of our biological nature and as essential to our evolutionary success as promiscuous sexuality. The final word is also not in on the challenge to the "masculinist lens"[10] of evolutionary psychology by scholars like Fisher and Hrdy, who claim an evolutionary right to promiscuity for women as well. That claim would definitely upset Christopher, who became extremely jealous whenever he thought that his wife was receiving too much attention from another man. Which brings us at last, as any discussion of sexual infidelity must, to the subject of jealousy.

Is Jealousy a Blessing or a Curse?

A sea change in both popular and scholarly ideas about jealousy occurred in the 1970s. The following description is by Robert Bringle and Bram Buunk, two social psychologists whose research has focused on jealousy:

> The prevalent attitude in society prior to the mid 1970s was that jealousy was not pathological at all; on the contrary, analyses of the writings in popular magazines in this period show that a certain amount of jealousy was viewed as the natural evidence of love and was good for marriage.
>
> Since the beginning of the 1970s, we have witnessed remarkable changes in attitudes toward jealousy among scholars as well as in certain segments of society. With the increasing emphasis on personal growth and autonomy in marriage and other intimate relationships—manifested in popular writings such as *Open Marriage* by George and Nena O'Neill— more and more people came to see jealousy as a deficiency in their relationship and as something wrong with themselves that had to be overcome.
>
> The view that reconceptualizes "normal" jealousy as being problematic has undoubtedly resulted in social psychologists being sensitive to the lack of knowledge concerning such an omnipresent and often overwhelming emotion. Most programs of research on jealousy of which we are aware started around 1974.[11]

Have we been wise to fully "reconceptualize 'normal' jealousy as being problematic"? What about older notions "that a certain amount of jealousy" is the natural evidence of love and good for marriage? Despite the transformation in social attitudes about jealousy, the actual relationship between jealousy and either personal or interpersonal adjustment has not yet been defined by a convincing body of research. It is not even clear if there is any consistent relationship between them at all. Changing attitudes about jealousy have stimulated ongoing research; they do not reflect a more advanced state of scientific understanding. Certainly, feelings of jealousy are a fairly universal aspect of human experience. A more positive language for these feelings is a concern for exclusiveness in a relationship, which begins to appear in children's friendships at about age ten. An emphasis on exclusiveness emerges just as children seem to develop an awareness of time as an important dimension to friendship: they begin to hope that a friendship will last and to notice its fragility.[12] In other words, jealousy goes hand in hand with caring about what happens to a relationship over time.

Four hundred years ago, Shakespeare personified the tragedy of intemperate jealousy in the character of Othello, who murders his faithful wife in jealous rage. Just last week, our local newspapers reported that a doctor was arrested after he entered his estranged wife's hospital room and shot her lover to death with a revolver. Clearly, any defense of jealousy must be a moderate defense and must place great emphasis on phrases like "a certain amount of jealousy." We offer such a defense, since it follows naturally from our ideas about tidal drift and the need for an alarm system in lasting relationships.

Recall Jennifer and Harold Sorenz (and Robert) from Chapter 1. We said that Harold suppressed his uneasiness about Jennifer's drift away from him and her increasing involvement with Robert, her fellow law student. The portion of his "uneasiness" that centered on Robert was clearly jealousy, and Harold felt very uneasy about being jealous. He completely agreed with the contemporary view that feelings of jealousy reflect insecurity, poor self-esteem, and selfishness. He was certain that they revealed his pathology rather than his love. So he kept quiet, never sounded an alarm, never called Jennifer back. Soon she was gone. Yet there is a safe distance and a clear distinction between saying something such as "I hate how much time you're spending with Robert; it's starting to change things between us" and heading over to Robert's apartment with a revolver. It is the difference between loving concern and pathological possessiveness.

Sharing Spreads like Ripples from a Stone

It is important to let the alarm of jealousy be audible in a marriage because of a curious ripple effect that can be set in motion by an experience of sharing or closeness. Karen Prager, a psychologist, has attempted to develop a more precise language to describe relationships.[13] She defines close relationships as "those characterized by strong, frequent, and diverse interdependence." She distinguishes closeness from cohesiveness ("the togetherness, sharing of time, and sharing of activities in a relationship") and intimacy (sharing that is "personal"). Her attempt at scholarly precision makes important distinctions between types of sharing, but the common, sloppy, interchangeable usage of words like closeness and intimacy also reflect a profound folk wisdom: when two people share something important with each other, there is a natural tendency for that sharing to spread into other areas. People who work closely together on a project over time begin to confide in each other, to share aspects of their personal lives as well as their work, to care about each other. (When caring does not develop, they usually manage to bring about an end to the working relationship as quickly as possible.) People who care about each other can easily begin to care in ways that are both loving and sexual. The old boss-secretary liaison was not based solely on the predatory nature of men. One historic attempt at a solution (although only for heterosexuals) is the segregation of men and women in separate work settings. In its absence, the best defense for a couple who want their relationship to last is an awareness of sharing's tendency to progress, a willingness to exercise a bit of caution, and a comfort with the expression of "a certain amount of jealousy" as part of their shared effort to sustain the natural ebb and flow of closeness.

In addition to a distance alarm within a marriage, we need a closeness alarm outside. Jealousy in modest doses can serve as an early warning system that safeguards a relationship by alerting the partners before they find themselves "getting in too deep" with someone else. Of course, for most people, the crucial measure of depth is sex. That fact, obvious from experience, was confirmed by study of a diverse sample of 250 Dutch persons:

> The results showed that behaviors that involved some erotic or sexual component, such as flirting, petting, and sexual intercourse triggered much more jealousy than other behaviors, even when these other behaviors included a rather high degree of intimacy with a third person, such as talking about intimate matters. Not only is intimacy with a third person that occurs outside a sexual relationship not as likely to arouse jealousy as when it occurs within such a relationship, but sexual relationships without emotional intimacy were found to evoke more jealousy than intimacy alone.[14]

Although this research-based conclusion may seem like unnecessary proof of what everyone already knows, the quote also points to something "illogical" about our jealousy. The behaviors that make us most jealous are not inherently those that represent the greatest threat to our relationship. When sexual jealousy leads to the end of a relationship, it is usually precipitated by the "betrayed" partner. By contrast, the "betraying" partner is probably more likely to seek divorce because he or she feels better understood and more cherished than because the sex is so good. A jealous focus on sexual fidelity is more logical from an evolutionary perspective, where the goal is preserving DNA, not preserving loving relationships. Using the evolutionary argument as a foundation for personal choice and social policy is a bit tricky, however; it seems to provide equal support for both promiscuity and murderous revenge against promiscuity. If, however, we take as our personal goal the preservation of a loving relationship, we may want to use our intelligence to tinker with our "natural" responses.

At the moment, the idea of tinkering with natural responses like jealousy seems very much out of fashion. So much genuine intellectual excitement is generated by our emerging understanding of the powerful effects that biology in general and genetics in particular have in shaping our behavior. There is a strong temptation to respond to that picture with a fatalistic shrug—our responses are simply how we must respond, unless we alter them with medicines. Although we should certainly feel humble and sober as we confront that emergent understanding, it would be a tragic mistake to sacrifice our ability to make at least *some* choices on the altar of biological determinism. Many individuals in marriages or other committed loving relationships somehow manage not to have affairs. Many couples manage not to destroy each other or their relationship even if some jealousy-engendering drift has occurred. An understanding of ebb and flow in relationships, along with an appreciation of the ripple effect of sharing, can both increase the odds that we will be faithful and also make a marriage more resilient when faced with an act of infidelity.

Reasonable Jealousy

The first step is to shift the "distance alarm" of jealousy from its current exclusive focus on sexual behaviors to a more general willingness to express concern about other forms of extramarital involvements that seem to be generating a drift apart. Perhaps that shift is not actually so unnatural. There is significant variation across cultures about what behaviors trigger jealousy. Contemporary culture has exaggerated the distinction between sexual and nonsexual sharing and defined sexual sharing as the only legitimate basis for jealousy. Cheating has become one-dimensional; its only dimension is sex. Not all societies have defined the grounds for jealousy so narrowly. The goal of that narrowness is unquestionably worthwhile: to provide greater autonomy and personal growth for each spouse. Since nonsexual involvements outside marriage are by definition not a threat to the marriage, they can be freely pursued. Many times, in couples' therapy, the statement, "But there's nothing sexual going on" is supposed to end the discussion, no matter how much time and how much intensity the speaker is sharing with a third person. As much as we would like it to be, it's just not that simple. We are not proposing a return to constricted lives for couples who want their relationship to last or a grim marriage based on suspicion and a short leash. We recommend a greater attentiveness to the risks of progressive intimacy outside the marriage and to the ebb and flow of closeness within it. It is important for someone to feel free to express concern about a drift apart, even if that drift seems to have nothing to do with sexuality. It is important for both partners to appreciate that sufficient shared time, shared activities and shared intimacies are essential to periodically restore a movement toward each other.

A surprising cause of nonsexual drift apart can be the decision of one spouse to enter individual psychotherapy. Paradoxically, the drift can occur even when the treatment is begun for the sake of the marriage. A psychotherapist can easily seem like an ideal version of what we want but do not always get from a spouse. Here is someone who always listens attentively, seemingly undistracted by any other concerns, working so hard to understand and be helpful. The situation becomes even worse if patients start to hide their most intimate worries in order to save them for examination in psychotherapy. Sometimes we assume it would be a misuse of our closest relationships to "impose" our innermost troubles on a spouse (or friend or other relative). Sometimes a spouse will encourage that belief, relieved to be able to shift the burden of those worries to the psychotherapist. Yet if we stop sharing what matters to us most with a spouse, the relationship soon becomes devitalized and hollow. Our spouse begins to feel peripheral and not of much help. These are not good feelings in the long run, even if they offer some short-term relief. A drift apart has begun. It is often exacerbated by the misguided idea that what is discussed in psychotherapy should not be discussed with anyone else. Yet this drift can be easily remedied with a little healthy curiosity and perhaps even a touch of reasonable jealousy about what is happening in a spouse's psychotherapy.

We share some of the modern mistrust of jealousy, however, so we will quickly balance a call for more jealousy with one for less. It is important to distinguish between jealousy's positive function as an early warning system and the destructiveness of unforgiving bitterness about past offenses. Given the certainty of periodic drifts apart in any relationship, no matter how loving, and the naturalness of slipping toward someone new during those drifts, a willingness to forgive a spouse's slips, including perhaps sexual ones, can also safeguard a marriage over time. Obviously, this path is a dangerous one to follow and can lead to great pain and regret. It can also at times be the only way to avoid the unnecessary destruction of something precious.

Sometimes, a person may seem to be forgiving only out of inertia or a failure of nerve. Despite the relative ease of divorce in recent decades, the writer John Taylor offers an accurate observation in his account *The Story of One Marriage:* although it "requires will to make a marriage work, it also requires a horrifying act of will to make one end."[15] On the other hand, sometimes it takes a crisis for us to remember how much another person means to us. Ellen Berscheid, a social psychologist who has written extensively about love, suggests that "people in smoothly functioning, emotionally tranquil relationships will underestimate the importance of their relationship and the intimacy it provides."[16] If jealousy can awaken a couple from that carelessness but not be allowed to destroy their relationship, they can once again begin a movement toward each other.

The slowly disintegrating marriage of Emily and Tom Harris illustrates the danger of listening too attentively to the alarms of jealousy and also the costs of ignoring them too completely. Tom grew up in a small New England town. A little awkward, a little shy, he was an easy target for family jokes and for his father's episodic rageful contempt. When he finally left home for college, he was astonished to find that, far from being incompetent, he was exceptionally talented as a mechanical engineer and he fell in love with the process of designing elegant solutions to complex manufacturing problems. He was equally surprised to discover that he was attractive to women, dated a number of them, and fell in love with Emily. Their youthful exuberance and carelessness led to her becoming pregnant. The wedding was less an expression of their love than a response to the demands of two angry families.

Yet they clearly did love each other. A combination of jealousy and obliviousness to it kept their marriage from ever reflecting that love. Two years into the marriage, in which Tom had been repeatedly tormented by the thought that he had not freely chosen to get married, he spent a weekend with an old girlfriend and made love to her. He was seeking some way to understand what he felt for the girlfriend and for his wife. That was his only sexual infidelity in thirty years of marriage. He returned to his wife more committed to the marriage and confessed to her. Over the subsequent twenty-eight years and the rearing of three children together, Emily never forgave him or trusted him. He was forever, in her eyes, the unfaithful husband. She was forever deprived of the pleasure and contentment that Tom's subsequent loyalty might have offered her. Certainly, this is a cautionary tale about the catastrophic impact that even a single sexual betrayal can have on the trajectory of a marriage. Tom's faith that his confession would be received in the spirit of marital renewal was at best naive and at worst self-absorbed and self-serving. After all, Emily was burdened by her own misgivings about beginning a marriage with a "shotgun wedding." Tom's words only seemed to confirm her worst apprehensions. But their story also illustrates the destructiveness of an unrelenting jealousy that cannot move on, either to a renewal of intimacy or an actual separation. Instead, jealousy froze the natural movements of closeness into a tortured still life, with decades of bitterness that deprived both Emily and Tom of either comfort or relief from the other.

There is another dimension to this unhappy story, however. Tom was joyously engrossed in his work. He loved the moments when he could transform an intricate problem into a simple solution. He loved proving wrong the father who had ridiculed him as inept. When he was caught up in a project, the hours would vanish unnoticed. He would arrive home late and leave early the next morning, filled with obvious enthusiasm. Emily suspected an affair with a female colleague with whom he worked closely. He assured her that there was no sexual attraction at all, just collegial respect and affection. No sex, therefore no problem. "Enlightened" modern thinking supported Tom's innocent obliviousness to what was on the mark about Emily's jealousy, even if she was wrong about the sex. The same thinking interfered with Emily putting her finger on the important nonsexual aspects of her jealousy: Tom shared more time and more excitement with his coworker than he did with his wife. The marital connection was relatively impoverished. Emily felt she did not have the right to complain about that impoverishment in anything but sexual terms. Tom felt that as long as he was sexually faithful, he had no need to make other adjustments in his life for the sake of his marriage. Tom was ignoring the importance of shared time and shared passions in a marriage. Emily was sounding an alarm about the continued distance between them. Yet, because nonsexual jealousy is treated as unsuitable these days, they never had the right discussion and never made any changes that might have begun a new movement toward each other. If Emily had been able to be a little less relentlessly jealous about Tom's weekend of unfaithfulness twenty-eight years ago and if both she and Tom had been a little more attentive to her jealousy about how he spent his time, even though he was not having sex with anyone else, their lives might have taken a very different path. A better balance between sexual and nonsexual jealousy, however unfashionable and perhaps unnatural, might have saved them from decades of a bitter and cold marriage.

After thirty years of unhappy marriage, the Harrises began couples' therapy with the declaration that they both loved one another. They meant it. Two individuals who are in love can nevertheless be mismatched in so many ways. They can differ in how much intimacy they need to feel comfortable, in how much time they must spend together to feel close, in how much their sense of connection depends on intimate conversation and how much it requires touching or making love. Because people differ in their primary modes of connection, one person can genuinely feel warmly engaged with a partner who at the same moment feels that their intimacy is ebbing away. That is why it is so important to listen carefully to a spouse's alarms. When Tom spent an extra hour at work before returning home, he honestly did not feel that he was diminishing his closeness to Emily. Yet he was. During that hour (and all the others like it), she felt that he was drifting away and she in turn pulled back from him. She told him but he did not believe her. He reassured her that he was not in love with his colleague, but those words were not the reassurance she needed. She needed more of his time.

4

Typical Early Milestones
Falling in Love, Marrying, and Having Babies

> It has been said that marriage is the remedy for the disease of
> love, a remedy which operates by destroying the love.
> **Willard Waller, *The Family: A Dynamic Interpretation***

There is nothing more exciting than falling in love. Throughout
the ages, poets, artists, and novelists have tried to capture the intensity of feeling and heightening of perception that arise when love
"strikes." A singer declares:

> I hear singing but there's no one there
> I smell blossoms and the trees are bare
> All day long I seem to walk on air,
> I wonder why, I wonder why.

The final worldly reply is:

> You don't need analyzing.
> It is not so surprising . . .
> You're not sick you're just in love.[1]

Love's intensity makes all other states of mind seem less real to the
lover. Love's intensity makes love itself look a little unreal and very peculiar to a disinterested observer. The effort to evoke that strangeness
leads cynics to use words like sickness and disease (or in an earlier time,

magic potions and Cupid's arrows). Psychiatrists have sometimes described falling in love as a normal experience of mild psychosis in which none of a person's usual commonsense understanding of the world seems relevant to someone "possessed" by love. The saying, "All's fair in love and war" trumpets the general belief that ordinary rules and expectations are suspended when someone has fallen in love.

What are the ingredients of this glorious but agonizing state? Poets have probably supplied the best lists, but we will focus on one particular ingredient: the euphoric avalanche of emotions that go along with intimately discovering another person and becoming intimately known yourself. The leap into intimacy is a very risky business and may feel at times like bungee jumping. There is both intense anxiety and intense relief in peeling away layers of disguise from yourself and from the other. In *The Transparent Self*, the psychiatrist and writer Sydney Jourard argued that there is a basic human need "to make oneself fully known to at least one other significant human being"[2] and, when that need is stymied, malaise and maladjustment result. But it takes time to make oneself truly known, time and courage, for the process carries with it the terror of revealing something that will drive away the other forever.

A usually outgoing twenty-five-year-old patient recently described his frightened, blissful muteness at a dinner party, seated near a stunningly beautiful woman whom he had admired silently for months. What could he possibly say that would be worthy of *her* attention, that would not make him sound foolish and destroy his hope completely? Leo Tolstoy, the Russian novelist, gives a wonderful description of that same terror when Levin, a major character in *Anna Karenina*, catches sight of Kitty, the young woman he loves but has barely talked to.

He followed the path to the skating pond and said to himself: I must calm down, I mustn't be excited . . . What's the matter with you? What is it? . . . Be quiet, jackass! he kept saying to his heart. And the more he tried to calm himself, the more his breathing grew labored. An acquaintance saw him and called out to him, but Levin did not even recognize him. As he approached the ice hills, he heard the clatter of the chains dragging the toboggans or letting them down, the rumble of the toboggans, and the sounds of gay voices; a few more steps and the skating pond opened up in front of him. He instantly picked her out of all the skaters.

He knew she was there by the joy and the terror laid hold of his heart. She was standing talking to some woman at the opposite end of the pond. There seemed nothing special either about her dress or her attitude; but for Levin it was as easy to pick her out of the throng as a rose among nettles. Everything was lit up by her. She had a smile that made everything radiant round about. Could I go on to the ice, he thought, and go up to her? The place she was standing seemed an unapproachable shrine, and there was a moment when he was on the verge of leaving, he was so filled with fear. He had to make an effort and reflect that all sorts of people were passing around her, and he might have come there to go skating himself. He stepped down, avoiding a long look at her, as though she were the sun, but he saw her, just like the sun, without even looking.[3]

The terror of falling in love often arises, as it did for Levin, from the wish to imagine the other as perfect and the tormenting fear that one is not good enough to deserve that perfection. It also flows from the state of doubt and uncertainty that may be an essential component of passionate love. The psychologist Sharon Brehm postulates that passionate love can only exist under conditions of uncertainty, the state of "hope without possession."[4] There must be a sense of risk-taking and what Brehm calls the "terror of loss of hope"—the possibility that all could be lost with a false move. She quotes the nineteenth-century novelist Stendhal, who wrote a treatise on love titled *De L'amour*.

If one is sure of a woman's love, one asks one's self if she is more or less beautiful; if one is in doubt as to her feelings one has not time to think of her appearance . . .

Always some little doubt to calm, that is what keeps one ever eager, that is what keeps alive the spark of happy love. Since it is never devoid of fear, its joys can never pall.[5]

Obstacles to Falling in Love

If the person is too easy to attain, imperfect reality necessarily takes the place of the imagined perfection. The unfolding of reality cannot happen too easily or swiftly without shattering love's imagination. Not everyone has the capacity for loving idealization, however. Anxious people who have been disillusioned too early in childhood are wary of this crucial idealizing phase of love. Their radar is set to detect flaws quickly so they won't be trapped again in someone's thrall and set up for the same kind of disappointment that they experienced in childhood. Even when such people are infatuated, they use most of their energy searching for problems that will give them an excuse to leave.

The movement toward intimacy can also feel risky because we usually have worked hard to establish a degree of personal freedom and it is frightening to be on the verge of giving some of it up. Loving someone means being dependent on that person—accountable for your own actions and whereabouts; curious about and susceptible to the other's actions and whereabouts. Americans, who are part of a culture that puts so much emphasis on individualism and personal freedom, find "it difficult . . . to become intimate and loving with one another because they feel like they are giving up personal freedom and autonomy by being accountable" (in the words of sociologist Ann Swidler).[6] So falling in love has an additional danger—you can lose your hard-won independence by being answerable to another—making many people worry that they will regress to a childish state.

But what about the relief involved in finding someone to love? We were born as very social beings. When we watch how babies and toddlers respond to being separated from their caretakers, the reality of our mutual dependence literally screams out to be acknowledged. Through enormous effort by parents and the wider culture, children learn to *act* more independent but their need for company never disappears. Love offers the possibility of life-long company that is more protected from the dangers of fate and circumstance than most relationships. When lovers swear to be together "till death do us part," they are in part whistling against the coming blasts of the winds of fate. Young people who have moved out of their family home often feel homesick once the novelty has worn off—but they have no guarantee that they'll ever find or make another family. Falling in love offers the possibility that the limbo of life apart from a family will not go on forever. At last there is hope for a life plan that can be pursued jointly rather than in lonesome solitude.

The Emergence of Ebb and Flow

The psychologist Sharon Brehm[7] suggests that even the most intense re-lationships experience occasional periods of "aridity" that interrupt early passions. Sometimes the aridity is caused by the inevitable emo-tional exhaustion that must eventually succeed a season of such strong feelings. Sometimes the aridity follows an external event such as a de-pleting illness that creates a breach in the intense experience. In our schema, we would say that Brehm's aridity is a first appearance of the ebb and flow that will then form the ongoing pattern of a lasting rela-tionship. We can only feel so much before our senses go dead and we need to "refuel." This transient state that Brehm calls (again borrowing a phrase from Stendhal) the "dead blank" can lead a person in love to doubt the authenticity of that love. In reality, it is the consequence and cost of the euphoria and agitated despair that are central to passionate love. The depletion can be perceived as an ebb in affection. We must not misinterpret its meaning in this way. Emotional aridity appears uni-versally when we are too tired to sustain intensity any longer. In less pas-sionate states we remember the need to refuel (to sleep, eat, wind down), but in the state of new love, all those needs may easily be forgot-ten in the "electrical surge" of passion.

One widely shared intuition about passionate romantic love these days is that it won't last. The resigned acceptance in our country of an almost 50 percent divorce rate for the last thirty years has left many young people deeply cynical about love and its capacity to last over a lifetime. This cynicism makes a commitment to matrimony frightening, yet over 90 percent of Americans do eventually marry. Individuals who grew up in families where there was a divorce are most likely to combine an overromanticized vision of "true love" with a deep mistrust of any ac-tual love they encounter.

As the moment of solemn commitment approaches, panic sets in. One couple appeared for their first couples' therapy session just weeks before their wedding date, desperately seeking some advice or experi-ence that would help them decide whether to go through with it. Once again, we can look to Levin (the character in *Anna Karenina* that Tol-stoy felt was most like himself) to picture a man on his wedding day petrified with fear about the commitment of marriage and intensely suspicious of the appearance of love.

A strange feeling came over him. He was overwhelmed by fear and doubt . . .

"What if she doesn't love me? What if she is only marrying me because she wants to get married? What if she doesn't know herself what she is doing? She might come to her senses and only after she is married realize that she doesn't love me and never could love me."

And strange and most evil thoughts about Kitty began to come into his mind. . . .

He leaped to he feet. "No, this won't do!" he said to himself in despair.

"I'll go and ask her. Say to her for the last time, 'We are free and don't you think it's better than everlasting unhappiness, disgrace and infidelity?'"

In despair, he drove to her house despite the orthodox custom that a groom not see his bride on the wedding day until they met at church for the ceremony. He found her in one of the back rooms, sitting on a trunk, giving her maid orders for packing. She was surprised to see him.

"Darling, I mean why are you here? This is a surprise."

She dismissed the maid and turned to him.

"What's the matter darling?"

"Kitty, I'm terribly unhappy and I can't be unhappy alone. I've come to say there's still time. We can put a stop to it all and put it right."

"Put it right? I don't know what you're talking about. What's the matter with you?"

"I've said it a thousand times . . . I mean, that I am not worthy of your love. You can't possibly consent to marry me. Think it over. You've made a mistake. . . . You can't love me . . . if . . . I mean, you'd better say no. . . . Better now, while there's still time."

"I don't understand. Do you mean you want me to retract . . . that you don't want to . . . "

"Yes, if you don't love me."

"You're mad."[8]

So it is not unique to our time for a groom (or bride) to get cold feet on the way to the altar. Passionate love has always been a risky affair.

The Science of Love

The new "scientists of love" assure us that this state of mind has to do with brain chemicals like phenylethylamine that create feelings of elation, exhilaration, and euphoria. Phenylethylamine is a natural amphetaminelike compound. In combination with elevated levels of other neurotransmitters such as dopamine and norepinephrine, it seems to lead to the "natural high" of people who are enveloped by the euphoric state of love. Neuroscientists also are studying our sense of smell and the ways in which subtle chemical formations may touch off strong feelings of attraction in the "primitive brain" where the olfactory (smell) centers are located. As yet, however, no neurochemical studies address the course of love over time.[9]

Dorothy Tennov, a psychologist, has attempted to systematically study and describe the experience of being "in love," which she calls "limerence".[10] The condition starts when another person takes on a "special meaning." Once this occurs, "intrusive thinking" begins. Regular thoughts about the special person start to monopolize the thinking of a person who is falling in love and can expand to fill between 5 to 85 percent of his waking hours. Tennov next describes a process she calls "crystallization" in which the person is idealized *even though* the lover can list the faults of his or her beloved. The lover feels dominated by hope, uncertainty, and unmitigated fear, as we have already described. We call this combination of qualities infatuation when it begins and passionate love if it continues over time.

The First Year of Marriage

There are a variety of sociological studies that look carefully at what happens to passionate love, once established, over the first year or so of marriage, gathering information from couples through surveys and interviews. (Most surveys do not address the lag time between falling in love and taking marriage vows.) Back in 1938, Willard Waller, the forerunner of the modern "love researchers," described a process of decline in love in the first fifteen months of marriage in his classic book, *The Family: A Dynamic Interpretation*.

As the area of privacy diminishes, the opportunity for idealization diminishes at an equal pace. As intimacies increase, the opportunities for disquiet are multiplied. . . . It is of the nature of early marriage interaction to tend toward an unusual intimacy. . . . It is not surprising, therefore, that the honeymoon so often ends in conflict.[11]

He went on to say that "[First] gently and then with startling brutality, the real person and the reality of marriage pound at the portals of thought and at length enter." In other words, he felt that during that first year of marriage, idealizations are eroded by the petty realities of day-to-day life.

In 1986, researchers surveyed 168 couples in rural central Pennsylvania to find out how couples fared during the first fifteen months of marriage.[12] They interviewed each member of these couples at three months and then at fifteen months after marriage. A summary of their results includes the following: "All of the husbands' and wives' subjective evaluations of marriage show a decrease in their sense of satisfaction over time." Specifically, they all "felt less in love after a year of married life." Interestingly, wives were more dissatisfied with the couples' interactions than husbands were. The division of labor in these couples after marriage usually became more traditional; wives did most of the housework and cooking while husbands did more repairs and outdoor work. "Another notable change is the dramatic reduction in the extent to which marriage partners say and do things that bring pleasure to their spouses; similar drops occur in the extent to which spouses show their affection by hugging, kissing, or having sexual intercourse." It is important to note that, in spite of these important declines in love and satisfaction, the changes were subtle and in general the emotional tone was still highly positive after a year of marriage.

In the same study, there was evidence that bad interactions have greater power to undermine a relationship than good interactions have to repair it. During the newlywed period, the more in love a couple felt, the more affectionate they were. One year later, the amount of affectionate behavior did not correlate much with the marital attitudes of either husbands or wives. By contrast, the amount of negative interaction a couple had early in the marriage predicted their continued negative interaction a year later. A more recent study[13] has shown that for newly-

weds, the amount of affectionate expression a husband gives his wife re-
duces the effect of his negativity on her marital satisfaction. After two
years of marriage, however, a husband's affectionate behavior no longer
had the same buffering effect. Apparently if a husband is too critical, the
wife simply becomes fed up regardless of how loving he is at other times.
(It is intriguing to note that wives' expressions of affection did not
buffer their negativity toward their husbands even as newlyweds.) John
Gottman, a research psychologist, has quantified this effect. In recent
studies of couples who were headed for divorce, he found that when a
couple exceeds a ratio of one negative exchange for every five positive
exchanges, they are headed for trouble.[14]

In summary, researchers have found that the first year of marriage is a
hazardous time in which the excited pitch of passionate love often declines but usually does not die. After a year, there is still a sense of novelty and wonder for many couples, but it is tarnished by the stresses of
making a life together and adjusting to the other's habits. There is evidence from the National Center for Health Statistics that the divorce
rate following the first year of marriage is exceptionally high.[15] Conflict
and disillusionment during the first year of marriage can lead directly to
the end of a relationship. Nevertheless, fighting is sometimes essential
for spouses to effectively communicate to each other which issues really
matter to them in the long term. When early fights fulfill this commu-
nicative function, conflict often decreases after the first year of living
together.

The First Decade of Marriage

Another research group extended the view over the first nine years of
marriage. They found that scores in the Marital Adjustment Test declined for the first three years and three months of marriage and then
leveled off.[16] There was no further decline in *average* scores, although by
the nine-year mark, 20 percent of the couples had decided to divorce.
Maybe we have been led astray by the memorable movie title, *The Seven
Year Itch*. The first low-water mark of closeness seems to be the third or
fourth year of marriage.[17] Evolutionary psychologists have proposed an
explanatory theory: three or four years is the time it takes for a child to
be securely weaned from the breast. After that, parents can separate

without harm to the child. It is a fairly weak theory, however, since children remain a significant burden on parental resources well past age three or four, even in the most primitive cultures.

Whether the fundamental cause of this initial ebb is our biological nature or the collapse of love's idealization in the cold light of everyday intimacy, most people are acutely conscious of the change because the first rush of passionate love is so vivid in both partners' memories. What most people are not aware of is the naturalness of an ebb-and-flow pattern in long-term relationships. They assume this decline is a one-way street and give up on behaviors that express curiosity, interest, and affection for their lover. The possibility of renewing curiosity in one's partner by embarking on joint projects or getting together regularly to talk about the changes that are happening in each person's inner world gets lost. Instead, most people start to feel bogged down by the logistical complexities of everyday life and work, and the spousal relationship gets short shrift.

What happens when this picture is complicated by the birth of a first child? The contemporary view is that if a marriage is in trouble, the last thing in the world a couple should do is have a baby to renew their closeness (in contrast to older advice to do just that). Yet most young couples report that having a child is the most astonishing thing they have ever done together. Many women and men with fascinating careers and lives of adventure feel that none of their exploits bring either the breadth or depth of pleasure and pain that they discover in having children of their own. No matter how much they have heard about the stresses and strains of parenthood, new parents are continually astounded by the seeming uniqueness of their own experience. When a couple decides to have a child during the first few years of marriage, it actually gives them the chance to start a whole new chapter in their lives, to embark on a joint project that potentially infuses their shared lives with new meaning and purpose. Why is it that for some couples having children achieves that end, whereas for others it breaks the back of a relationship that is already losing its vitality?

Questionnaire-based research suggests that most couples have a decrease in marital intimacy and satisfaction after the birth of a child. In general, wives seem to experience a more steep decline in satisfaction these days,[18] [19] [20] probably because the problem of balancing child care with a paying job is so impossible to solve that mothers are left feeling guilty most of the time. The average husband reports a smaller but still measurable decrease in marital satisfaction. Psychologist Karen Prager summarizes current research on young parents as follows:

> The transition to parenthood seems to hasten a decline in adults' intimate contact with other adults, whether spouse, friends or parents. Because of the 24-hour per day demands of new babies, parents may find themselves curtailing all activity except work and infant care, including sleep. Because they are consumed with the parenting task, young adults also devote less attention to the quality of their marital relationship and friendships.[21]

A crucial factor in whether or not the birth of a child damages or strengthens a marriage is the attitude that a couple has toward parenting. When the couple approaches raising a child as a joint project in which each parent needs to bond with the child and play a crucial role in child care, the novelty of the experience has the potential to make the couple feel satisfied and fulfilled like no other. There are some studies that support this view. New mothers with the most supportive husbands have fewer problems during pregnancy and less postpartum depression. Couples who are most happily married share more in parenting. Mothers may take care of children regardless of the quality of their marriage, but the better the husband-wife relationship is, the more fathers participate in child care. What emerges is a picture of a circular process. A better marital relationship leads to a father being more involved in child care, which leads, in turn, to a better marital relationship. Obviously, there can be a vicious circle in the other direction that leads to increasing disengagement.

In 1992, we conducted a small pilot study of thirty middle-class couples looking at how wives and husbands balanced the roles of child care and work.[22] It also provided interesting information on how marriages change with the birth of a first child. All the participants were astonished by how much time, effort, and money raising children seemed to take. In general, they reported less "fun" since having a child but a much greater sense of satisfaction and sense of purpose to their lives. Some quotes from the study interviews capture the mixed feelings couples had about how their life together had changed.

Here is a forty-four-year-old father, a scientist with two children ages four and fifteen months, answering the question, "How has your relationship [with your wife] changed since you've had children?"

It certainly has changed. For one thing, it's made us more stereotypic in terms of role division, who does what, more so than it was before there were children. And that has taken some adjustment. It's practical. It has to be that way. So there's been that change. We obviously have less time to spend with one another and to have fun with one another. But I certainly feel that the magic is still there in the relationship. There is a closeness that wasn't there that was brought on by having some kids in the house and the work that's involved in being together. We've worked very hard at being consistent and I think we both pride ourselves on being able to do that, in presenting a unified picture to the children, so in some ways it has brought us much closer.

His wife, a teacher taking time off while the children were young, gave the following response to the same question:

We used to spend much more time doing fun things together. We were always a good . . . we worked together as a team and I think that basically continues, although I think that having children, the differences in our style become much more obvious. So that's changed. We're sort of able to give to each other much less. And the other way it's changed is that I'm working less, so I'm not the wage earner I used to be, so financially my husband has taken on more of the burden of the family. That's a big one because I think he feels the strain of that. . . . I would say we have an excellent relationship. I feel very, very satisfied. I feel that we really work together. I think we really like each other. And we've had so many years together. I look forward to retiring with him, and when it is just the two of us again and that we can go back to doing what we used to do. And I think, I mean it's hard, but I also think we work hard to maintain that relationship. It doesn't come so easily, it's just not like that. We do things to take good care of it.

Another woman described the changes in her marriage since having children as follows:

Oh, yes; we used to spend a lot more time just being by ourselves, a lot more quiet time and we'd do a lot more things together. There's a lot less time to talk on a day-to-day basis, consequently a lot more sense of pressure. Like the Thursday nights when we have dinner together, filling one another in on the whole week plus talking about the children which we never have time to do and talking about what's going on in our own lives, talking about my mother who needs more talking about now that she seems older and more dependent; so there's a lot more dependents in our lives, people who depend on us more. It's interesting because I think there is a lot of struggle around mutual dependence that my husband and I have for one another. We used to be much more mutually dependent on one another. Now there are so many people who are dependent on us that we sort of have to put up a strong facade, and it takes its toll I think in terms of warmth and closeness between us. That is, we're so strong for other people that we can't let down some of the guard so we wind up being more cool and aloof toward one another. We can break down but it takes some doing. And it takes arguments sometimes and just sort of concerted effort sometimes, and sometimes just talking about it. But we have to catch ourselves being sort of automatons rather than flesh and blood human beings. Sometimes with our schedules, being a flesh and blood human being is tough.

This woman does a wonderful job of describing the difficulty in a marriage with children of getting off "automatic pilot" to allow a husband and wife time for genuine closeness. As she says, it takes "concerted effort" to get out of productivity mode when both members of the couple have such difficult schedules. Even if a couple puts time aside once a week for talking to each other, the time is often used to discuss the complex problems of all those who are depending on them. Their "special" time together may end up as just another extension of the productivity mode that the couple is always in. The interest in each other and inquiry about each other's most intimate thoughts that was effortlessly present during the infatuation period may disappear altogether until a sense of leisure returns, which may not come about until after they can discuss all the necessities and still find time left over for each other. On the other hand, these parents and most of the others in our study were eloquent in describing the sense of purposeful mission that they have in this phase of life.

Here is one woman's response to the question, "What are the most satisfying and least satisfying aspects of family life?"

> Well, the most satisfying are, they're both the same thing really. When it works, I think, My God, I'm pulling this off, this is so great. I'm having this research career, I have this wonderful family life. I love my husband, I love my daughter, she's fantastic, this day care's so great. They're taking such wonderful care of her and I feel what more could I possibly want, this is so perfect and great. And then, you know, the very next day she can have an ear infection and I can be having a hassle at work and I'll feel like everything sucks and I'm just shitty at everything. I'm a bad mother, I'm bad at my job, I'm a lousy wife, everything sucks. It just happens so quickly, it's really like you're on a roller coaster and you've just got to hang on. And I wasn't prepared for those types of things or those types of feelings. You know I've worked so hard to get myself on an even keel in life and then to finally get there, have a baby and then find out you're on the gigantic roller-coaster again is amazing.

Even though these couples miss some of the fun they shared before they had children, there is now a sense of meaning to their lives that knits them together. They are in the "through thick and thin" part of the marriage. But like many couples, they sometimes let the time devoted to re-creating closeness between them get too thin in their relentless pursuit of maximum productivity. We have found that all couples occasionally make the mistake of assuming that the relationship will take care of itself even if there is insufficient time for intimate communication. Often they only realize this mistake after one of them has begun to feel estranged and sounds the alarm.

Friends Outside of Marriage

There is another sector of life that suffers when a couple has children and, although the effects on marriage are indirect, they are significant.

Many parents find they no longer have sufficient time or energy to connect with adult friends and relatives. The problem is amplified when both parents work, as they do in 60 percent of families currently. Quite a few couples in our study reported that hectic schedules and their commitments to children, spouses, and jobs left precious little time available for seeing friends. Here are the responses from both husband and wife in one couple to the question: How have your relationships with other people (than your spouse) changed since you've had children?

> Husband: It's almost difficult to sustain relationships with other people. Your friends tend to be parents of your kids' friends. I think I'm a lot more non-sociable as a consequence of that. . . .
>
> Wife: I also have much less time, much, much less time for friendships. I have a few friends I'm close to but these are very few . . . you know I still know people but it's very hard to keep contact and sometimes that is very hard to take, especially in hard times like when I'm depressed or something and I look around for my friends and we don't have time to develop real deep friendships and it's very hard to cope when you have problems, so I feel isolated a lot because we run to work, we run home, and then we do it again.

In this couple, both parents worked full time and their three children were in school or day care. We found that when both parents had full-time jobs outside the home, there was a sense of so much to do that the time available for socializing was in danger of vanishing. Without at least one parent working less than full time, there was no one to take the initiative and arrange get-togethers with other adults or families. It became clear that most couples in the study had a hidden set of priorities: children first and then each person's paid job. Other priorities such as seeing friends, seeing relatives, time alone as a couple, and religious activities seemed to come after children and work. Unfortunately, other concerns can easily drop off the list altogether because there is so little time left.

Explicitly, the goal may be to place children and marriage first, but when any of these apparently secondary priorities is forgotten, even for a while, some of the marriage's foundation may crumble. Marriages flourish best when woven into a larger tapestry that includes extended family, friends, neighbors, and peers. If most couples are knocking themselves out to make ends meet and provide the necessary economic support for the family,[23] there is little energy left for making sure that the couple and family are an active part of a community. Without that sense of context and witnesses, a couple can feel so isolated that there are few social forces working to keep the couple together. We will return to this important topic later in the book.

The Value of Ebb-and-Flow Theory

So how does our theory of the ebb and flow in close relationships apply to the early phase of committed relationships? How can an understanding of the fact that relationships are always drawing closer or further apart help a couple's movement past the predictable milestones of these years? The first few years of any long-term, intimate relationship is the time when a series of precedents are established for reconnecting (or not) after periods of drift apart. The initial waning of idealization and early passion almost inevitably creates a sense of drift. If two people are to reconnect, especially now that most spouses work in separate settings, they must appreciate the need for private time each week to permit the verbal and physical sharing that a relationship needs to flourish. During this private time, there must be proper respect from each partner for the ways in which the other prefers to be close. This may mean that a husband needs to engage in intimate conversation before sexual closeness, even though his preference might be the opposite. Or to move directly to touching when he would rather start with an account of his day. Similarly, a wife might need to take a path to intimacy that is different from the one she usually prefers, for example, having sex before intimate conversation. Both partners might also have to understand that their notion of intimate conversation might be quite different from the other person's, which must be respected too. If an external pressure interferes with the couple's usual private time for reconnecting, each person needs to recognize the likelihood of slight feelings of estrangement on both sides, even though it was nobody's fault. As we discussed in an earlier chapter, the "rustiness phenomenon" that makes people feel shy, awkward, and irritable after absences can set in very quickly, sometimes after reconnecting time has been ignored for only a few weeks.

Moving into Parenthood

The ebb-and-flow model also has important implications for the transition to parenthood. Couples who experience an ebb in closeness after the first few years of a committed relationship are also partly responding to the loss of novelty in what had been an incredibly novel and exciting journey. In the preceding chapter, we looked at how some people seek to recapture that novelty and excitement through a new love affair. It can also be recaptured by falling in love with a child who is born or adopted into the family. If the time with the new member of the family is clearly much more one parent's task than the other's, however, this seemingly safe source of novelty turns out to have some of the same dangers as an illicit affair. With a new child, we advocate a kind of "ménage à trois," a parenting model in which the glorious adventure of nurturing a new life is shared by both partners so that neither feels left out, jealous, and bitter. Since both parents are not equally blessed with milk-bearing breasts, the father may have to be "engineered" into a major role in early parenting so that his chance to become engrossed and bonded is almost as great as the mother's. But the bond between the parents also needs to be attended to, even in the excitement of the earliest months of a new child's arrival. It is so easy for a couple to feel sexually estranged, especially when a woman already feels like she is sharing precious bodily fluids with her brand-new smaller partner. The distance created by the birth of a new child is in fact a danger point in many marriages. Both partners need a maturity they may not easily feel when they are sleep-deprived and worried about loss of income; the husband has to channel his sexual needs into enjoying the physical closeness with his brood (wife and child) and the wife may have to remember not to take her husband's ability to nurture himself too much for granted.

Progressive drift apart is also more likely if a couple has no other adults to talk to and get help from. Adult friends can be a boon to marriage. They help protect a couple from an overly pressured, claustrophobic feeling in their marriage and they also can provide respite periods away from the new child for a couple to be intimate with each other. When couples with newborns tend to avoid seeing old friends and relatives, we worry that they are making a strategic error in terms of their own relationship. Not only are they endangering the safety net provided by a community of friends and extended family, but they are also avoiding one of the main sources of help with the monumental task of childrearing. It is true that an affluent couple might be able to hire help for child care, but such help will not necessarily be available in emergencies, like the assistance of a relative or friend. Our American antipathy for obligation and our curious unwillingness to depend on anyone unless we pay them has isolated us too much as we gain in affluence; the "self-sufficient" nuclear family is cracking under the strain of too much pressure to serve all of each member's needs.

During the first few years of a relationship, both members of a couple must remember that, if "the bells aren't ringing" in quite the same way as when they fell in love, it means nothing about the viability and sturdiness of the relationship over the long haul. Over the first three or four years, a relationship has to change, especially with all the pressures on it from the outside world and family life. For a relationship to stay healthy, there must be tolerance for the ebbs and flows along with a commitment to display the ongoing curiosity about one's partner that encourages reengagement, even though one may assume (usually wrongly) that one can predict exactly what he or she will say. If each person is always on automatic pilot, sure that the other has nothing new to share, it will become a self-fulfilling prophesy . . . and soon each partner will start looking for someone who will find them new and fascinating.

Probably the best defense of that commitment to ongoing curiosity appeared in a reply by the columnist Judith Martin (Miss Manners) to a husband whose wife was reading at the dinner table. Here is the reader's question and Miss Manners's response.

Dear Miss Manners:

Years ago, my wife and I agreed that we would not read at the table during meals in what I thought was an attempt to eliminate a bad habit developed during our single lives.

So when my wife started recently reading at the table during meals, I objected. She asserted, I think accurately, that she can read and take part in the conversation. I, on the other hand, tend to get absorbed in what I am reading to the point where I frequently do not respond to comments addressed to me. Therefore, my wife asserts, it is not OK for me to read at the table.

Actually, I don't think this is about manners. I frequently do not respond to my wife's comments when they are not in the form of a question or I do not have a ready response. My wife complains that when I do not say anything, she does not know if I have heard her.

I understand her point and try to do better, but I am not perfect. I think each failure adds to a heap of disappointments in a marriage that may have had more than its fair share of stress. A counselor's office would be a better place to resolve this issue than your column, but she won't see a counselor and I am not yet prepared to threaten to end our marriage in order to get her to one.

As we are trying to teach our children good manners, I would appreciate your thoughts on reading at the table.

Gentle Reader: Miss Manners does think this is about manners, which is to say that she considers the situation more serious, not less than ordinary marital strain—even a large share of ordinary marital strain. So you have come to the right counselor.

First she will deal with the etiquette rules.

1. It is rude to read at the table when someone else is present, and being able to converse as well doesn't make it any less rude. The insult consists of saying symbolically, "I'm bringing my own entertainment because I sure don't expect much from you."

2. It is rude to greet another person's remarks with silence, even if no question has been asked. The insult consists of saying symbolically, "What you say is not interesting enough to warrant any acknowledgement."

At this point, Miss Manners hastens to disabuse you of any notion that she has slyly led you to what a different sort of counselor would say—that the solution lies in better communication.

On the contrary. She knows perfectly well that there are times when the most recently purchased George Eliot novel has a great deal more to say than even the most beloved of husbands, and that the most interesting wife in the world is, like everyone else over the course of a lifetime, bound to deliver a great many unremarkable remarks.

What you need is politeness, which is to say the respectful pretense of interest in each other. Your wife should arrive at the table as if she expected you to be interesting, and you should respond to whatever she says with an encouraging noise, if only "Oh really?" or "Hmmm."

The deeper manners issue here is that neither of you is willing to make an effort to be polite to the other. The only solution would be to make that effort and hope that the show of interest and respect will rekindle the real thing.

Miss Manners' approach of dealing with the surface rather than whatever lurks beneath it will seem less eccentric if you think of how you want to teach manners to your children. As parents, you probably know that they love you—and yet you also know that they are often bored senseless by much of what you wish to say to them.

If you allowed them to express the boredom, it will make the whole household unpleasant. And if they are not taught to feign interest in other people, no one else will want to establish a household with them.

Miss Manners, in her effort to remind us of the purpose of politeness, does a wonderful job teaching what many couples therapists would agree is a useful lesson. If husbands and wives bring into their marriage some of the skills they have already mastered in dealings with new acquaintances and friends, an ailing marriage may start to flourish again. If instead they assume that none of the listening skills perfected in public social interchange belong in a marriage once spouses know each other well, they are in trouble. Although Miss Manners claims to be dealing with the surface, she recognizes that feigned interest allows real interest to emerge. Turning away when closeness has waned does not.

The first few years of romantic relationships are usually the most exciting and the most hazardous. The unfolding process of getting to know another human being well and becoming known thoroughly in return is an amazing journey. It holds the promise of relieving the existential loneliness of every human being. But it puts us at the mercy of a series of vicissitudes that mark all human interactions—the movement back and forth from closeness to distance that is the hallmark of lasting relationships. If one does not have this pattern in mind, the trip may seem even more improbable and hazardous because the swiftness with which feelings of closeness can disappear and be replaced by a sense of alienation catches one off guard. That alienation is sometimes circumstantial, as when geographical distance and time (or perhaps a baby) interfere with the rhythm of regular reconnection. Sometimes the alienation begins with an emotion, as when a person's feelings are hurt or siphoned off by some unusual preoccupation. But it is the nature of relationships to encounter these interruptions in closeness and the ongoing task of couples who want their love to last to compensate for them regularly so that intimacy is maintained. If, over the first few years of marriage, a couple establishes a rhythm of reconnection following the inevitable drifts apart, they will be well positioned for a long journey together.

5

After the First Decade
The Middle Years of Marriage

Most people see their lives as stories, and the story has to move
forward.

Dan McAdams, quoted in the *New York Times*

A t their best, the middle years of marriage are like the middle of a
novel that we cannot put down. We are carried along by the momentum of a story that has taken hold of our imagination, our curiosity,
and our sentiments. The recently released report from the MacArthur
Foundation's project on midlife development offers a hopeful picture of
these years:

> The majority of middle-aged Americans reported that their marriages were
> stable and relatively happy. Ninety percent agreed that it was not very
> likely or not likely at all that their relationship would eventually break up.
> More than half responded "never" when asked how often during the past
> year they thought their relationship was in trouble.[1]

These are couples in the thick of their life stories, separate individuals
who have come to see their lives as intertwined dual stories. Consciously, they have no plans to cut them short. This news would be even
more heartening if we did not have to reckon simultaneously with a

very high divorce rate among these optimistic couples. Many individuals who have no particular plans to end their marriage end up putting it at risk "by accident," lulled into carelessly taking it for granted as an abiding fact of life.

One man in the middle of a good marriage was Paul Benton, an engineering professor who supplemented his university income with consulting jobs in other cities. He hated the extensive travel that this work required, however. He yearned to be more involved in his family's day-to-day routines, and he loved his role as father to a three-year-old girl. His wife Joan also worked, but she had arranged her hours as a software engineer so that she could be home after school and on most weekends. Paul often felt irritated with Joan because she never seemed to appreciate how hard it was for him to get on a plane and be away from the family for days at a time. He would get lonely and anxious sitting in an airport waiting for yet another plane and sleeping alone in hotels.

On some of his consulting projects, Paul worked closely with a woman in his department named Anne Lintel. Because they had worked on joint consultations successfully, they began to be requested as a team. Soon Paul started to spend more and more time with Anne even when they weren't at work, confiding in her and sharing his worries. He was more open about his anxieties with Anne than with his wife. He didn't want to be a burden to Joan and feared she would see him as a wimp rather than a strong, stable provider. Thus, his friendship with Anne deepened as he felt increasingly known and comforted by her. The next thing he knew, it had become a physical relationship that then moved, almost imperceptibly, from physical affection to sexual consummation.

Paul started to dwell more on his irritations with his wife, above all, his feeling that she put too many people and obligations ahead of him on her priority list. Denigration of one's spouse during an affair is a common guilt-relieving move. It helps justify the affair and can ease a move toward separation. But, deep down, Paul did not want to endanger his marriage and risk losing his family. Anne also did not want to place her own marriage in jeopardy. They started living a double life, trying to have the best of both worlds but greatly increasing Paul's anxiety. Clearly, Paul's story is quite common. It is even common among men who are in the midst of vital healthy marriages. No doubt, some of the 90 percent of middle-aged Americans in the MacArthur Survey who thought it was not very likely that their marriage would end will eventually have similar stories to tell.

The important news is that a large portion of affairs start in marriages in which both partners report that they are quite contented. Once someone begins moving closer to another person outside the marriage and is headed toward a sexual relationship, it is difficult to halt the momentum of infatuation and excitement. To ease the conscience, the errant spouse must start to believe that there were already major defects in the marriage or else the affair would never have happened. Our culture's emphasis on "one true love" doesn't help matters any. The implication of this romantic fallacy is that one could never possibly be attracted to a "second true love," certainly not to the point of acting on it, while in a happy marriage. The reality is quite different from the myth. It is quite possible for someone to love or at least care immensely and romantically about two people at the same time. Each mother awaiting the birth of a second child cannot imagine loving the second as much as her first. Yet she is regularly and happily surprised to discover that she comes to love the second equally. We are all very capable of loving more than one person romantically if we let ourselves. Yet we risk losing much that we cherish when we do. The middle years of marriage may be especially risky in this regard. The marriage is anything but new and we tend to take for granted a relationship that has lasted so long.

Everyday Heroism

For a marriage to survive and flourish in the middle years, it helps to have a notion of everyday heroism—the sustained commitment to noble but ordinary goals. William Kilpatrick, in his book, *Why Johnny Doesn't Know Right from Wrong*, seeks to win dignity and glory for what he calls "the hero of everyday life":

> The difference between the hero of legend and the hero of everyday life may be put this way: For the traditional hero such as Ulysses or Jim Hawkins the adventure takes place away from home. Home is where you

go after the adventure. For the average adult, on the other hand, home *is* the adventure, the place where he lays himself on the line. The adventure consists precisely in those commitments with which the classical hero or child hero rarely allows himself to be entangled. The temptation for the traditional hero is to avoid the adventure and settle down; the temptation for the ordinary hero is to avoid commitment and have an adventure. For the ordinary hero it is staying home that is the hard thing, the thing that requires courage and energy. He must put aside the child's fantasy of escaping. Once having accepted the main adventure, he cannot allow himself to be distracted.[2]

Kilpatrick offers Frank Capra's movie, *It's a Wonderful Life*, as a superb story to convey the importance of everyman's day-in and day-out commitment to ordinary responsibilities. George Bailey, the central character, is a good man overwhelmed by despair as he faces, through no fault of his own, scandal and financial ruin. He is a man who has, with great but largely silent effort, subdued his yearning for adventure to fulfill ordinary responsibilities in an extraordinarily dedicated way. He is saved from suicide by a lovable angel who shows him how things would have been for his wife, his friends, and his town if he had never lived. By this device, George regains a sense of meaning in his life and viewers, who identify with him, see a type of heroism that is largely invisible from day to day, yet unmistakable when his life is viewed as a whole.

Unfortunately, there is not enough positive feedback from society to sustain today's everyday heroes in their "calling" as parents and spouses, struggling to balance seemingly irreconcilable demands and dreams. Instead, men and women are expected to become "self-actualized" through a career, whereas child rearing and marriage are supposed to be pursued without credit or applause, yet nevertheless done superbly on the side. Mothers of these women rarely give them accolades for their diligent strivings to combine career and family because the mothers themselves often sacrificed careers to do a better job of raising their own children. Fathers have trouble complimenting their adult sons who help in more egalitarian child rearing because they may then end up looking bad themselves for not changing diapers and giving baths years before.

A Child-Centered World

Currently, parents who strive to combine ambitious careers with the everyday heroism of raising children often try to compensate for their arduous work schedules by organizing a child-centered home. This approach can easily backfire in a variety of ways, even though it is launched with the best of intentions. First, it may lead to very selfish children who expect the world to revolve around them and become enraged or demoralized whenever it doesn't. Second, overindulgence may lead to children who are so demanding that their parents begin to stay at work even longer than necessary because home has become more than they can manage. Sociologist Arlie Hochschild studied the daily lives of employees at a mid-American corporation and reported the results in her book *The Time Bind*.[3] Many employees, but especially women, worked longer hours than were necessary because time with their families left them feeling emotionally depleted. Hochschild believes that when both parents work outside the home, there is a "third shift" of "emotional work" (after outside jobs and the basic labor of housework and child care) that each parent is too drained to take on. Nicholas Lemann describes the results in his *New York Times* review of Hochschild's book:

A cycle may develop. Home, because it is continually shorted, keeps getting messier. Sullen children, resentful spouses, inconvenient stepchildren, elderly parents and manipulative exes lurk there. Relationships at work, which get the nourishment of time, become deeper and richer.[4]

Often this cycle is perpetuated and amplified by parents who alternate between guilty overindulgence and depleted avoidance.

Third, too exclusive a focus on children during limited time at home may lead a couple to give each other short shrift. It is an old dilemma that warranted an earnest motherly warning in Louisa May Alcott's *Little Women*.

You have only made the mistake that most young wives make—forgotten your duty to your husband in your love for your children. A very natural and forgivable mistake, Meg, but one that had better be remedied before you take to different ways; for children should draw you nearer than ever, not separate you.[5]

A contemporary update to this venerable advice would add that fathers too can be so enchanted by their children that they neglect their wives. We can be sure that when a couple starts feeling estranged to the point of contemplating separation, the children are almost always devastated. Given the choice, they usually would rather give their parents more time "alone" than worry about whether their parents will stay together. But children do not give up attention easily. At times, parents need to plot and plan to keep some private time together so their relationship does not wither from lack of contact.

One article on the lighter side of this problem appeared in the *Ladies' Home Journal*.[6] Called "Sex, Lies and Videotapes," the subtitle is "Dying for time alone with your husband? Take it from me, Desperate times demand desperate measures!" Melinda Marshall describes her strategy to protect weekend mornings from her children's intrusions. The children (ages eight, seven, and three) are typical, affectionate tykes who would love to spend weekend mornings cuddling and playing in their parents' bed. Marshall and her husband, deprived of time for lovemaking or intimate talk, devised the following plan. They eliminated TV totally during weekdays. They allowed their children to watch cartoons only on Saturday and Sunday mornings and showed them how to get their own cereal breakfasts. Finally the father declared, "So guys, keep the sound down, huh? Any fights, any screaming—you settle it yourselves, okay? Because if Mom or I have to get up, the TV goes off." Marshall continues, "That put the fear of God into 'em. We've had near perfect compliance." She also devised another ruse. She packed the youngest child off to Grandma's and allowed the two oldest to camp in the backyard in a tent. She told them they would not be allowed to stay out all night because she knew they weren't quite ready yet. They of course begged and pleaded. Soon the parents had a whole night of privacy in the house. Obviously, most parents might not be so creatively devious. Actually, most parents are so tired from their multiple obligations that they just let their sexual life fall to the bottom of their priority list. In this resigned way, the problem of low sexual desire has become the most fre-quent sexual difficulty that brings people to sex therapists in the United States today.

Parents who feel it is selfish to take time for themselves as a couple need to remember the following: a healthy marriage is one of the most loving presents that parents can give to their children. Not only does it offer them a positive picture of family life that they will hopefully be able to draw on when they come of age; it creates an atmosphere in which they can develop and flourish without having to worry about the state of their parents' relationship. The swing of the cultural pendulum has carried us far in the direction of too much work and too much indul-gence of children, with comparatively little time for adult relationships (in remarkable contrast to the amount of writing devoted to the sub-ject). The pendulum swing is in part a reaction to certain near-sacred rituals of an earlier generation, such as the cocktail hour in which chil-dren were expected to stay out of the way while their parents unwound and conversed about the day. Now there is precious little sacred time for couples who have children. Even the family supper, the traditional cor-nerstone of family life that at its best succeeded in balancing attention between adults and children, is disappearing because the time to prepare and share it is so hard to come by. Of all the factors eroding family life today, overlong work hours for both parents may turn out to be the most pernicious.

Another important feature of marriage in the middle years is that most individuals find that they have less time for friendships than at any other phase of life. In a study we conducted ten years ago, men were most likely to report loss of contact with friends during these years. As women work increasingly long hours, however, the problem has extended to both genders, despite the fact that women have historically attended to adult friendships with greater dedication than men. Unfortunately, it puts too much pressure on the marital relationship if husbands and wives must satisfy all of one another's wishes for adult intimacy because friend-ships have dropped out of the picture, lacking sufficient time and atten-tion to sustain them. In an earlier book, *Overcoming Loneliness in Everyday Life*, we recommended that during the child-rearing years, cou-ples engineer into their lives the cooperative sharing of child care with other families.[7] Cooperation between families offers the possibility of new friendships and intimacy that grow out of the demands of family life rather than battling against them because of limited time. This approach may end up compensating for the loss of the extended family in the same way that "false kin" did in the American South during the eighteenth century. There, adult relatives were so often dying before children came of age that a backup network of caretakers known as false kin became a regular part of the social system. When "give and take" is engineered into family life through sharing tasks like child care with friends or neighbors, a marriage is strengthened by taking pressure off the husband· and wife to manage *all* adult responsibilities within the family, both physical and emotional. We will explore the complex interactions of friendship and marriage further in a subsequent chapter.

Couples Without Children

How are the middle years different for couples without children? There is certainly a little more time for processing what is actually happening in the relationship and making adjustments along the way. There is perhaps a greater sense of "steering" the relationship in ways that represent active choice. There also is less of the unquestioned sense of purpose and meaning that children can give to a marriage. Couples without children have to pay much more conscious attention to creating a sense of shared meaning in their life as a couple. When they have been involved in a joint project or mission that comes to an end, they cannot just let things carry on without planning a new chapter or adventure. Without ongoing recommitment to shared activity, they risk a growing sense of malaise. Children may not eliminate these challenges, but they frequently delay them. In the middle years, couples without children experience a series of crises of meaning in the relationship that couples with children have the luxury of postponing until the "empty nest" moment arrives. Drift is an even greater danger when the traditional notion of marriage as an institution to create and nurture children is replaced from the start by a more personally defined commitment. If two partners then drift toward parallel lives, there are no children to draw them back together, to reengage them in a compelling, long-term joint project that always needs tending.

On the positive side, however, couples without children have the possibility of freely pursuing their dreams without constantly worrying about whether their actions will hamper the development of their young. In fact, studies show childless older adults report higher marital quality than couples with children, especially in the areas of intimacy and mutual respect.[8] Perhaps they are better off in old age because they have had more time to maintain social networks throughout their adult lives rather than needing to rebuild them as children get older. Perhaps there is also an advantage in facing mini-crises of shared meaning along the way rather than suddenly confronting a major one when the nest empties.

Many childless couples find that they wish to take on causes or "callings" to fulfill their nurturing instincts. Some take on leadership roles in their extended families. Others seek careers that give them a chance to nurture or mentor younger colleagues. Still others adopt beloved pets and let the world of animals replace the world of children as the domain of their parenting needs. It is worth remembering the research on the nursing home residents by social psychologist Ellen Langer: those who had plants to take care of lived longer and reported greater contentment than those who had nothing to care for.[9] We can only conclude that humans were meant to care for something, be it animal or vegetable.

Many gay and lesbian couples offer good examples of long-term childless relationships embedded in a community that places less emphasis on parenthood than many other groups. Connected to a network of similar couples, they are less likely to experience the isolation that some heterosexual childless couples suffer surrounded by friends and neighbors in the thick of child-rearing. Gay and lesbian couples have described to us how much they cherish the freedom to take on causes or to go on trips without the impediment of children's schedules. Yet they also describe feeling cheated of the experience of parenting, viewing it as yet one more social deprivation imposed by a homophobic society. It is a deprivation that more and more couples are unwilling to accept, driving one of the more divisive controversies of contemporary life. It is interesting to speculate whether "gay" might disappear as an inclusive term for homosexuals as homosexual couples with children become just as driven by the demands and chores of child-rearing as heterosexual parents.

Whether a couple is homosexual or heterosexual, however, taking on joint projects is likely to lead to a journey together that is both more exciting and more intimate. Sharing similar interests is not quite enough. Whether the project is child rearing or something else, it must require activity and effort from each partner. Barbara and Rob Burnett, a fashion designer and photographer, respectively, had supported each other's work for years. Each was proud of the body of individual work that the other had created, but often their projects carried them far away from each other. Rob tended to get overinvolved with some of the women he photographed, whereas Barbara's projects required faraway travel and late hours as she designed her new line of clothes. Each ended up feeling spurned by the other's devotion to work. Discussing their estrangement in couples' therapy, they recalled that their relationship had started twenty-one years ago when Rob did a fashion shoot of Barbara's designs for a magazine. The romance of sharing a project was something they thought they could reclaim. Soon they were traveling to the same site for another shoot and sharing the best of their creativity with each other rather than their colleagues. As they worked together for the first time in twenty-one years, some of the old excitement started to flow through their relationship again.

Transitions in the Middle Years

The middle years of marriage are often shaped by unexpected transitions that impinge on most people's lives. Just as in chess, the middle game is harder to characterize than openings or endings. Typical surprises might include the illness of a close relative, a period of unemployment, or a return to school by one spouse to prepare for a career change. Any of these transitions can quickly escalate into a crisis. An illness can progress to death or disability. A job loss can turn into an extended period of unemployment, with depression complicating the picture. Even a mother's return to paid work after staying at home with young children can assume crisis proportions because it changes almost every aspect of a family's functioning.

We have found that couples who most gracefully weather the ordinary crises of the middle years have an intuitive appreciation of four principles that provide them with resilience in times of major transition. First is the principle of the nest egg, a concept that can usefully be extended to more than money. A family must understand that, in the ordinary course of life, emergencies occur that demand extra time, effort, or help—or even just a little extra goodwill. It helps to be able to draw on reserves in all these areas, not just financial ones. A couple whose life plan depends on everything going smoothly will be paralyzed by anxiety whenever a possible crisis rears its head. Generating a flexible reserve of time to respond to crises, such as the illness of a young child or an elderly parent, is particularly hard in our work-driven culture. But much of the inflexibility is internal. Though we expect employers to understand our need for time off, self-employed people frequently have the most trouble permitting themselves extra time in a family crisis. The habit of going to work no matter what the family circumstance has become an expectation even for women in the workforce. Certainly a standard nest egg of money set aside for emergencies makes it easier to take time off. But other kinds of nest eggs can be just as important in a crisis—an employer's (or a customer's) goodwill, a network of friends and relatives who can help out, a spouse with sufficient reserves of understanding to tolerate the extra irritability, anxiety, or worry that comes with stress.

Then there is the principle of give and take, a process that helps to create nest eggs of goodwill. If one is regularly helpful to friends, family, and neighbors, an emergency in one's own family is much less daunting because those that were helped will be there to help too. Learning how to ask for help and not feel intimidated by the idea of being in someone's debt is difficult in a culture that overemphasizes self-sufficiency. It is impressive to see how crises are dealt with in extended families that have kept up their ties and the old-world traditions of give and take. Lois Roleto, a fifty-one-year-old married woman who lived in a suburb of Boston, was struck by amyotrophic lateral sclerosis (ALS, or Lou Gehrig's disease) when she was still in the prime of life. Her husband, Joe, their two sons, and her four siblings (who all lived in the Greater Boston area) were overcome by grief once they understood the awful finality of the diagnosis—the disease is invariably fatal. Lois had been very much the family matriarch since the death of her parents two years before, but soon her siblings took charge, investigating ALS on the World Wide Web and finding out all that could be done to make a patient's inevitable deterioration less miserable. They obtained equipment that allowed Lois to write words on an electronic message board when

talking became too difficult and let her communicate with other patients on the Internet.

Each sibling also found a way to raise money for the American ALS
Association; for example, one sister who was a hairdresser arranged a
cut-a-thon at her hair salon. Lois's relatives made sure that she had several visitors every week. Neighbors and friends supplied so many frozen
suppers that her husband never had to do any cooking. As she got worse,
her family gave their word that, no matter how ill she became, she would
be allowed to die at home. When she was very close to death, the hospital staff kept their word to the family and she returned home to die with
her family surrounding her. The medical staff continued to remark on
the strength of this extended family's ties, as well as the outpouring of
love for Lois. She had been as strong a force approaching death as she
had been in life. Lois was a person who had always "been there" for her
family and friends, so it was not surprising that everyone tried so hard to
be there for her. It was not just the power of one individual, however.
Lois nurtured and was nurtured in turn by a family culture that emphasized flexible give and take based on current needs and treated the extended family's resources as a shared nest egg to draw on in a crisis.

The art of pacing is a third area in which the most successful couples
are usually strong. These men and women seem to have a sixth sense
that lets them know when they have too much on their plate. When the
family or couple needs more "downtime" because connections are fray-
ing or basic chores remain undone, they responsively prune back outside
obligations to focus on essentials. It may be that just one member of the
couple has a good enough alarm system to recognize when they are
growing apart or that the home "infrastructure" is crumbling. He or she
may have to remind the other that something has to give. Experts in
pacing routinely organize their schedules to create some flexibility in
each week for the usual "unexpected" mini-crises that are a part of ordinary life: a dog that needs to visit the vet, a car that needs to visit the
mechanic, a spouse who is upset by a bad review at work.

The art of pacing includes recognizing that people need to go slower
when something objectively depressing has occurred. Every society has
created special rituals around grief and mourning. Our society seems to
demand that they be finished in the blink of an eye. If an aging parent
dies, most adults expect themselves to go on with the whole show,

hardly missing a beat, but mourning quietly on their own so as not to bother anyone. This is often unrealistic. It is similar to expect oneself to function normally eight weeks after a major operation no matter how you feel, simply because the doctor said you would have an eight-week recovery. In *Care of the Soul*,[10] Thomas Moore stressed the importance of acknowledging depression, learning from it, and nourishing one's soul with whatever the experience of depression has to teach. This is certainly an unfashionable idea nowadays. To do so, one must slow down. Many people would prefer to take themselves quickly to their nearest psychiatrist and get treatment. Whether or not one chooses to seek treatment, depressed mood (to be distinguished from a full depressive syndrome with physiologic effects such as changes in sleep, appetite, energy level, and capacity for pleasure) is a normal reaction to certain life events and it does slow one down.

Depression (whether mood or syndrome) is also an important cause of social withdrawal, so it can create a powerful drift apart in a couple. Even when a spouse is alert to the possibility of depression after a distressing event, depressed people tend to reject help and look angry and glum enough to discourage even the most solicitous spouse. But let's suppose that a person could say to his or her partner, "I'm depressed because my mother just died so I know I'm going to be hard to deal with for a while. Please try your best not to take it personally, and I'll try to make it up to you when I come out of it. And as soon as I feel I can talk about it better, I will." A spouse could in turn say to the children, "You know that Grandma has died. Often when people go through a death of a person they love, they aren't themselves for a while. They're more irritable, more quiet, more preoccupied. That's the way we are when we're in mourning. Crying helps too. But Dad will be back with us after a while if we give him some time to himself." The discussion might even help children to understand more about the mourning process in themselves. By contrast, the famous actress Katherine Hepburn, in her memoir, wrote about the toll it took on her family when no one ever said a single word about her brother's suicide during her teenage years.

The art of pacing comes into play during those times when a spouse's energy is being drained away by extraordinary concerns, whether depression intervenes or not. Pacing in this case often means being tolerant of the other person's change in pace. One partner may have to do more to protect a distressed spouse's right to slow down and be sad. This might mean relieving someone from usual chores. Or perhaps letting a spouse go on long walks alone while the other is watching a child's soccer game or getting the groceries. But only for a while, since our old worries about progressive drift are a concern here too. If a depression seems not to improve, the well spouse might have to arrange a referral for evaluation and treatment (and not infrequently insist that the appointment be kept). Nevertheless, the idea that life events, with their mix of practical and emotional demands at inconvenient times, will sometimes slow us down is one of those simple truths that seems curiously ignored when we look at everyday behavior.

Finally, some couples have a knack for keeping lines of communication open yet still knowing when to let something go and adapt. It might be called the Ecclesiastes principle: there is a season for talk and a season for quiet accommodation. To return to the example of a grieving spouse, sometimes quietly picking up the slack without complex inquiries into everyone's state of mind is just what the doctor ordered. Yet, in the long run, a couple must keep discussing their feelings about life events and changes, even when the feelings are hard to talk about or seem not to need discussion. If they stop talking, eventually a partner starts to feel like a dimly known stranger. The estrangement may be masked for a while by a comfortable assumption that often creeps into the middle years of marriage: after being together for so long, of course we know what a spouse is thinking. It's a risky business, however, and usually we are caught up short.

A Typical Milestone in Many Marriages

One of the most typical life transitions during the middle years of marriage is the moment when the parent who has been primarily responsible for child care returns to work outside the home or to school after the children have reached school age. No matter how ordinary this transition, it represents a massive change for each family. If regular open communication has disappeared, this transition can be particularly hazardous. It has become especially difficult in our time because husbands and wives are flying blind. Often each person came from a family in which their own parents fit the definitive fifties model—the mother stayed at home and the father worked full time. Even today, of course, the mother is almost always the primary caretaker and it is her return to outside work that most families face. When that moment comes, husbands are now expected to help more with every aspect of home life and mothers are still expected to do the lion's share at home, somehow managing to balance a part-time or full-time work schedule with continued primary responsibility for housework and child care.

This pioneering effort takes its toll on most families today. Wives, who feel they are already running as fast as they can, frequently complain that their husbands are hypercritical of almost every aspect of their housework. This serious tension is created by two small but powerful details in a major social transformation. First, husbands are in a position to look much more closely at the home front now that they are being called into action there. Second, these men were usually brought up by women who took pride in their housework because it was the only domain in which they were permitted to exercise their skill and creativity. The result is a generation of husbands who use their parents' world as a domestic gold standard and find their own homes too messy.

Husbands are now expected to support their wives' pursuit of a career with none of the complex and ambivalent feelings that their fathers might have had. In fact, although many men welcome help from their wives in producing family income, they may not look forward to their wives' absence from the home as a completely positive step. Though most men now begin marriage assuming that their wives will work, it is easy to settle back into more traditional roles after a few years of a wife at home with the children. The woman, meanwhile, is usually experiencing her own mixture of trepidation and guilt as she prepares for reentry in the "adult world." Each parent is likely to feel terribly irritable with the other as they cope with their separate anxieties. The ebbs and flows that continue to develop from week to week may no longer get the attention they need when each parent is so preoccupied with the momentous logistical changes in the offing.

Here is what one couple had to say one year after the wife's return to school to enter a nurse-practitioner program. The Klausmans have been married for eleven years. During most of that time, Anne was at home with their two children, ages eight and ten.

ANNE: I think that me being in school, aside from just the time issue, has represented a threat to our closeness over the time here and there. I think Herb has even talked about that. Yes? Feeling, you know, that it has been an adjustment to have me less available to the home and to have me more interested in something that has nothing to do with anyone here.

HERB: Well, it's that and also the notion that at the end of it, you will be financially independent and actually able to take care of yourself if there were to be a rift in our relationship, the reality that you could absolutely take care of yourself once school finished.

ANNE: Of course, I was always a nurse. So I always could take care of myself if I needed to.

HERB: Well, she's been very involved in her schooling. For instance, I went to law school. I closed my law books and I closed my shop at five o'clock and I'm done being a lawyer and I'm thinking about other things. Anne takes her schooling far more seriously than I ever took law school. I suspect she will take her job far more seriously than I take my job. . . . I suspect that things will change and not for the better family-wise. Anne will continue to grow and develop, and I bet she will be very substantial at what she's doing, and I think she's interested in being substantial at what she's going to be doing.

Clearly, Anne and Herb had all sorts of worries about this new phase of life. Both of them were genuinely surprised when these worries emerged during our research interview. Although each knew the other had complex concerns about Anne's return to school, neither really knew the substance of the other's fears. Generally content and comfortable in their marriage, they had simply begun to take for granted an intimate knowledge of each others feelings and go on with their increasingly complex lives. Unfortunately, old assumptions often do not hold in a time of change and it is easy to see how the Klausmans might have been headed for trouble. It was also a drift apart that they used our interview to correct. Even though they had been timid about telling each other their worries, the lines of communication were in good enough shape for them to be able to speak freely in front of each other when asked the right questions. Later in the interview, Herb described feeling like a burden when he would hint around that he wanted Anne to try to get back home in time for a family meal. He felt like a nag. Anne responded that his "nagging" was not a burden but a help and a comfort. It made her feel wanted and missed by the family. Sometimes, Anne said, she had to be "reeled in," back to her family and away from her studies. Herb was relieved (and surprised) to find that his hints were welcome and helpful when Anne felt herself getting carried away.

The Hazards of a Husband's Unemployment

Another harrowing time that many families unfortunately encounter in the middle years is a period of unemployment for the major breadwinner. If the major breadwinner is the husband, the practical problems of unemployment can easily be compounded by the couple isolating themselves from friends and relatives because of the strong sense of shame associated with men being out of work. Spouses can also become isolated from each other when shame inhibits open discussion within the couple or masks itself with irritability and anger. Wives who are working may feel bitter because they never expected to have to be the family's sole provider, even temporarily, and at the same time may be afraid that if they take credit for their position it will further damage their husband's self-esteem. Husbands may get discouraged because they fear that a new job will be impossibly hard to find and they will permanently lose their status both within and outside the family. They may also fear that speaking of these fears will simply confirm their inadequacy.

A little bit of depression is both expectable and dangerous because it makes it so much harder for someone to "sell himself" during a job search. In this situation, the mix of open communication and quiet adaptation becomes particularly tricky for a couple. The wife may have to put her own feelings of bitterness on the back burner and become a vocational coach in order to get her husband ready for rejoining the job market. The husband may have to put aside his embarrassment and get on with finding a new job. Dwelling too much on the crisis can easily

turn into destructive recriminations. Yet avoiding any acknowledgement of the swirl of feelings can create a devastating rift that never
quite gets repaired. Some couples may find that the subject becomes so
charged that they need a couples' therapist to help them talk safely and
objectively about it. A nest egg of goodwill in the marriage, however,
helps even more. So does a history of give and take with friends, neighbors, and relatives who can offer help (and maybe even job leads) in a
difficult time.

Dealing with a Preoccupied Spouse

As all these examples suggest, most of life's typical crises (like the death
of a parent, unemployment, or a return to work) affect one member of a
couple more directly than the other. Usually the more directly affected
spouse, even if not clinically depressed, will become preoccupied and
self-absorbed while trying to digest and process the new situation. He or
she may feel that this is just the time to let the relationship flow and
draw comfort from it but, because of sadness and preoccupation, cannot
remember how to make a spouse feel well-loved and nurtured. The "indirectly affected spouse" may do his or her best to be empathically
"there" for a while but eventually may run out of patience, feel more and
more abandoned, and experience a sharp ebb in affection or outright
impatience and anger.

The key is to get the preoccupied person's attention. Sometimes anger
works. Sometimes a "Heads-up!" is necessary to let the person know
that, in a family, going out of communication permanently is not an option. A reminder about the marriage vow to remain engaged with each
other "till death do us part" might be in order. If someone feels en-
trapped by an obsession, warnings or anger might help to blast them out
of a "stuck state." But it would be a mistake to think that a person in the
midst of grief is withdrawing on purpose. Children do a wonderful job of
distracting the bereaved from their sadness through persistent bids for
attention. Children do not often take no for an answer. Even if an adult
tries to stay in a withdrawn state, operating on a few less cylinders than
usual, children have the determination to get what they need, come hell
or high water. That stick-to-it-iveness is just what saves many children

of overwhelmed parents and leads to their resiliency, even in the face of parental depression. Adults need to recognize that partners may sometimes need a similar determination from us to reach them in their non-communicative state. Persistently trying to make contact, just the way a child would, is not necessarily a childish thing to do when an adult is preoccupied with a personal crisis.

Summary of the Middle Years

The middle years of marriage are a busy, productive time when most people feel their marriage is safe, since it has already weathered many years and milestones. Couples are apt to take each other for granted and to feel that they don't have to attend closely to a relationship once it has already stood the test of time. Complacency is an understandable but dangerous mistake. For many people, marriage is the "Rock of Gibraltar" that anchors all other major activities, projects, and aspirations. Following a divorce, these individuals are surprised to find how much their lives get stalled and for how long. Some undertakings that seem completely independent of marriage turn out to be exquisitely dependent on it, at least for much longer than most people think reasonable. For many couples, the marriage itself is each spouse's greatest asset, to be protected and treasured as such, yet its value can be missed most easily in the middle years, when its freshness is already gone and it has not yet gained the honor of distinguished age. Years of successfully riding the currents of tidal drift in a marriage may make couples cavalier. Their marriage may begin to feel as reliable as the tides. This is not the case. Drift, if it goes on too long, can lead to a marriage that feels dead beyond revival. If couples get into the habit of ignoring their anxiety over the drift, ignoring their alarm system, a perfectly healthy marriage can wither from lack of attention. The fact that a marriage has lasted a long time is no guarantee of its continued survival, particularly since divorce rates among the elderly, traditionally negligible, are on the rise.

6

The Comforts
(and Discomforts) of Age
Marriage in the Later Years

The participants in a workshop were given the following instruc-
tions: On a blank sheet of paper draw a straight line. One end of
that line represents your birth; the other end, your death. Draw a cross
to represent where you are now. Meditate on this for five minutes.[1]

Long before the five minutes are up, our metaphor of tidal drift col-
lides with the finiteness of our lives. The tides—or the oceans, or the
earth—will not last forever but they stretch far enough into the past and
the future to bestow a sense of timelessness on their cycles of change. As
a couple enters old age together, the ebb and flow of closeness continues, but it is dramatically reshaped by a new experience of time. When
young love's illusion of *forever after* becomes impossible to maintain,
both the time remaining and the time already shared by a couple take
on new meanings.

But first the statistical good news. Current research on marital satisfaction in old age has found that it is impressively high. The technical
word used to describe the course of marital satisfaction over time is
curvilinear: satisfaction starts high, decreases somewhat over the middle
years, and then rises again, especially with the departure of children
from the home. In one study of more than four hundred husbands and
wives over age sixty, 90 percent were happy or very happy with their
marriage; half of them thought their marriage was currently at its best.[2]

Older couples are likely to feel less passion but more contentment in their relationship. Emotional and romantic intensity decline, but so do negative interactions and overt arguments. Their contentment partly reflects a shift over time in what couples treasure about marriage. Individuals over sixty-five tend to evaluate the success of a marriage in terms of "survivorship (e.g., 'We've been married forty-five years—it's a good marriage'), shared experiences (e.g., 'We've been through the good times and bad'), and interdependence (e.g., 'We're a team—our relationship is good because we suffer together')."[3] Academic writings about love often distinguish between passionate and companionate love. Using these categories, we would say that, over time, couples tend to shift from passionate love to companionate love. Most couples are quite happy with the change. Or at least reconciled to it.

It is easy to feel skeptical about the stream of social science research that keeps telling us yet another phase of life that we once thought was difficult is actually quite sunny. Rebellious adolescents and midlife crises have both been swept off the path of normal development by recent studies. At least the quiet golden years of marriage were always as much a part of traditional folklore as the bickering old couple. These two dependable elements of ancient folktales and modern TV shows reflect crucial individual variations hidden behind statistical "facts." Yet long-lasting marriages probably are in better shape now than they used to be. A series of discouraging studies in the 1950s and 1960s found that marital satisfaction declined steadily with age.[4] Recent reports are much more hopeful (the "curvilinear" conclusion). A clue to the improved outlook comes from the "Middletown" studies of an anonymous midwestern town from the 1920s to the 1970s. Over the years, a major change occurred in how much communication between spouses was expected in a marriage and how much it was valued. In the 1920s, couples spent little time in conversation, bickered about shared decisions, and then "often lapsed into apathetic silence."[5] These days, not many couples, even older ones, easily accept an uncommunicative drift into sullen disconnectedness. Instead, the distance alarms go off and lead a couple to seek reconnection or else to separate. Since social, economic, and psychological barriers to divorce are lower, miserable couples are less likely to stay together. The unsurprising result is that couples whose marriages last tend to be happy with them. They also happen to be the couples who were happier to start with, since the best predictor of late-life marital satisfaction turns out to be the level of satisfaction in the early years of marriage.[6]

Surveys of marital satisfaction in aging couples are tracking a moving target. Patterns of marriage and divorce, the arrangements that adults establish to raise children, and expectations about intimacy and sexual fidelity continue to change with extraordinary speed. Today's studies of elderly married couples examine the effects of marriage arrangements established many decades ago. The problem for researchers is called the cohort effect: we cannot be sure if studies show the effect of the passage of time on marriage or simply show what marriage looks like in the particular generation that is currently reaching old age. Aging married couples have not only been married longer than their juniors; they married in a different era, with different beliefs and expectations. Yet each cohort's experience of lasting connections is shaped by the natural ebb and flow of intimacy.

Rebecca and Isaac Altman: Fifty Years Together

Isaac and Rebecca recently celebrated their fiftieth wedding anniversary, surrounded by their two daughters, their daughters' husbands, several grandchildren, and a small group of friends. On a marital satisfaction questionnaire, particularly at that moment, they would probably each rate their marriage as reasonably happy, just as they would have in its early years. It is a return of calm, however, after a tumultuous two decades that began not with the birth of their children but when their daughters settled down with families of their own in distant cities. Statistically, this is just when we would expect their marriage to begin to improve. Understanding why it did not sheds light on the obstacles that a couple must overcome to achieve marital contentment in their later years.

The Altmans were deeply involved with their children and committed to their children's professional and personal success, particularly Rebecca, who had given up pursuing a career as a sculptor early in the marriage to become Isaac's administrative assistant, overseeing his small biochemistry research lab. The long hours working together had left the couple thoroughly engaged with each other in a moderately successful shared enterprise, but credit flowed to Isaac, not Rebecca. By contrast, the nurturing of their daughters' development was a shared task in which Rebecca was the principal partner. Once the children were settled on their own paths, Rebecca shared a life with Isaac in which she felt increasingly unfulfilled and unappreciated. The work had not changed but its meaning had been reshaped by the passage of time. She was no longer building something to support the family she cherished. She could imagine the lab winding down over the next few years, retirement on the horizon. She felt a new bitterness, a troubling regret that she had not created something of her own.

There were two immediate consequences. Retirement began to assume momentous importance to Rebecca as a chance to redeem a life that she now felt had deprived her of creative self-expression. Retirement lacked the same importance to Isaac, who would have been content to noodle around with small research projects indefinitely. And Isaac became the chief reminder and cause of that deprivation for Rebecca, the prime target of her bitterness.

The Transition to Retirement

There are many theories and some survey-based research to help a couple like Rebecca and Isaac anticipate the effects of retirement on their marriage. The theories focus, reasonably enough, on the sudden increase in shared time that becomes available to (or imposed on) a couple in retirement. The most optimistic theories predict a "honeymoon" period of increased intimacy and affection that flows from the increased time together.[7] Financial planning advertisements capture this hopeful view daily with images of smiling couples enjoying blissful retirement activities together. A more nuanced view[8] suggests that realizing these dreams of low-stress retirement requires not only financial planning but good marital communication and compatibility. When these are lacking, in the words of psychologist D. H. Olson, "long hours together . . . may provide fertile ground for the reemergence of old issues and conflicts, or dramatically point up the lack of shared interests and values."[9]

These observations remind us that we need *both* shared time and shared interests to generate the periodic movements toward each other that sustain closeness in old age, just like any other time of life. Yet shared tasks and activities are equally important for rhythmic ebb and flow. Actually *doing* things together is not only the natural result of shared interests; it is vital to creating new interests that are shared. The cheerful advertisement pictures of retired couples bicycling together or walking along the ocean's shore holding hands assume that dreams are shared. All that needs to be done is to secure the financial resources that will let us live them out. Retirement, however, signals the end of a long period of agreed-upon tasks and roles in a marriage. There is no reason to assume that even the most contented joint participation in standard midlife enterprises like raising children, providing for the family, and building careers will automatically leave both members of a couple with the same vision for the next phase of life. New interests and enterprises must be found and, unless a couple is uncommonly lucky, negotiation and compromise will be necessary to make sure that some of them are shared. The need to agree on activities and dreams to fill the expanse of time ahead makes marital communication and compatibility critically important during the transition to retirement. A couple can no longer let their marriage move forward on automatic pilot, confident that the same arrangements that protected them from a progressive drift apart up to that point will continue to hold. The renegotiation also has a particular intensity and urgency to it: this may be the last set of dreams a person gets to choose.

It was that "last chance" urgency that preoccupied Rebecca—and separated her from Isaac who was much more content with the outcome of his "first chances" and felt no need for transformation. The two of them had worked effectively and closely over decades, riding out the inevitable hard times and periods of estrangement. They had arrived at the beginnings of old age fully committed to sharing it together. But they arrived there with different levels of contentment about the past, different desires for the future, and without the habits of comfortable communication that might have allowed them to re-create a shared vision without an explosion of bitterness, blame, and misunderstandings. They rode out this explosive period as well, although they might have separated if they had not both had an "old-fashioned" commitment to their marriage vows (more on this in a later chapter). They were also sustained at times by family members and a psychotherapist who acted in part as mediators, but perhaps even more important, as witnesses.

Marriage Without Witnesses

One of the great burdens of marriage in old age is simply the other side of the coin of spending so much time together. Along with loss of social connections in the workplace, the aging also face the loss of friends and relatives through death and health-related restrictions on their own mobility. The result is that elderly couples are significantly more interdependent and much less involved with friends and outside activities.[10] Just as socially isolated parents are more likely to abuse their children,[11] socially isolated couples are more likely to slip from an earlier code of behavior and drift into nasty or petty ways of behaving that they simply would not have permitted themselves in the sight of others. Although elderly couples need privacy for romance to thrive just as much as anyone else, keeping that privacy embedded in a larger social network can help keep fights from getting so mutually cruel that reconciliation becomes practically impossible. Rebecca and Isaac went through several stormy and painful years, but they never drifted so far apart that reconnection became unthinkable. Somehow, out of that cauldron, they forged a new shared vision of their shared life that let them pursue new activities together and separately (including Rebecca's reengagement with the world of art), without Isaac severing his ties to the lab completely.

Husbands at Home

Because the Altmans had always worked together, they did not face the traditional retirement crisis: the husband's sudden looming presence throughout the day in the home, which had previously been the wife's domain. In 1980, Norah Keating and Priscilla Cole published an article with the evocative title "What Do I Do with Him 24 Hours a Day? Changes in the Housewife Role After Retirement."[12] It was based on interviews with four hundred recently retired male teachers and their previously homemaker wives. A majority of the husbands but only 12 percent of the wives saw no disadvantages for their marriage in the husband's retirement. The disadvantages cited most frequently by women included decreased freedom, too much togetherness, and too many demands on their time. By contrast, only 4 percent of the men had regrets about spending too much time with their wives. For men, the major disadvantage of retirement was the loss of relationships in the workplace. Since the study interviewed recent retirees, we should not conclude that wives will remain perpetually unhappy with their husband's retirement. We can conclude that retirement forces a reworking and renegotiating of roles and expectations in a marriage and that the very arrangements that made a marriage successful during the working years may simply not work well in retirement.

Although Keating and Cole's results seem to stand on its head the usual notion that women want greater closeness in marriage than men, three other factors are probably more important in understanding why retired husbands are more content with greater marital togetherness than their wives. First is the issue of turf: imagine if a retired wife decided to spend her newfound leisure time hanging out in her still-working husband's place of employment. Second, Keating and Cole report that husbands rarely use their new free time to take over some of the burden of housework from their wives, although women's protective feelings about their turf make this more complicated than just male rigidity. Third, men tend to depend more exclusively on their wives for intimacy, while women more often spread a wider net of intimate relationships in which friends and other family members play a more important part. This difference may be why, as a group, widows are so much more resilient than widowers. All three of these factors make it particularly problematic when husbands retire first and wives continue their employment.[13]

The Burden and Comfort of Memory

So much must be reworked before a couple can be comfortable in retirement, particularly the balance between togetherness and separateness in pursuing interests, friendships, or even quiet contemplation. At least the leisure of retirement provides a couple with enough time together to have some hope of transforming decades-old patterns of dealing with each other. The explicit emphasis is on how to move into the future together. As we get older, however, more time is naturally devoted to looking backward, to reminiscing. How a couple faces their past together has just as powerful an effect on their sense of loving connection as their plans for the future. Rebecca felt estranged from Isaac not just because she wanted to attend art festivals while he wanted to hang around the lab. She was also separated from him by the weight of her past disappointments—and that weight can easily become a powerful club to bring to the negotiating table.

In youth, when disappointments and mistakes seem catastrophic, we need the comforting voice of experience to tell us that many things can still be set right. A carpenter friend of ours once explained the difference between a professional craftsman and a good amateur: the professional makes just as many mistakes but he is confident that he knows how to fix them. As we get on in years, that confidence peaks and begins to be stolen from us by the press of time. We no longer reasonably expect that we can muster enough effort, enough time, and enough luck to fix even the mistakes that matter most to us. We must then either find some way to be reconciled to our past or turn away from it, perhaps to distract ourselves with a flurry of new activities, with alcohol or drugs, or else fall into despair. When much of our adult lives have been shared with another person, that person is irrevocably a part of this process of reckoning, a thread and at times a motive force that runs through all our decisions and choices—our mistakes and regrets as well as our triumphs and satisfactions. Research on patterns of thought in individuals with and without depression have turned up a troubling but not altogether surprising fact: nondepressed "normals" tend to attribute successes to their own efforts or abilities and they attribute failures to external factors.[14] A crucial question as a couple ages together is whether one's spouse feels enough like a part of oneself to get credit for what went well rather than blame for what went poorly.

Inevitably, looking at one's spouse in old age will stir up at least some memories that are painful, some regrets about things gone badly or left undone that can no longer be remedied. We are tempted to look away from someone who reminds of us of our pain. Perhaps for that reason, the divorce rate among parents who have suffered the death of a young child is catastrophically high. What is to be done when a loved spouse is also a reminder of our regrets? How can that fact not push us toward a final drift apart in the later years of a marriage?

We must add one more shared activity to the list of projects that counter a drift apart. A couple must also be able to grieve together, to share regret, to come together in mourning. In 1925, the anthropologist Bronislaw Malinowski wrote that funeral rites serve to bind together individuals who would otherwise have a natural impulse to flee before the horror of death. The ceremony "counteracts the centrifugal forces of fear, dismay, demoralization, and provides the most powerful means of reintegration of the group's shaken solidarity and of the re-establishment of its morale."[15] His words also evoke the challenge to an aging couple confronting the "centrifugal forces" of disappointment and regret. Somehow, a couple must move from the private bitterness that builds walls to a shared regret that leaves each person feeling a little better understood, a little less alone, a little more cared about.

Paradoxically, the most common cause of private bitterness is the misguided loving wish to spare one's spouse unnecessary pain. Does Isaac really need to know that Rebecca feels she wasted her talents running his lab and wished she had lived her life differently? It's a little like keeping unpleasant secrets from children to spare them pain—a bit patronizing, probably not all that likely to work really well in the end, and perhaps sparing the secret keeper as much distress as those who are apparently being protected. Motives get confused in these situations. Keeping bitterness private not only protects the other; it also lets us secretly nuture our bitterness and protect it from any challenge the other might offer (for example, "But Rebecca, don't you remember that I begged you not to give up your art . . ." or, "Damn it, I also had dreams that I gave up for the sake of the family.")

Yale law professor Stephen Carter has written about the distinction between honesty and integrity.[16] Honesty that hurts the other person at no cost or risk to oneself is not a very impressive demonstration of integrity. He offers the example of a man who, after fifty years of marriage, confesses to his wife on his deathbed that he was unfaithful thirty-five years earlier. Honesty in the service of what goal seems to be the question. Rebecca could use her unhappiness about the road not taken as a kind of torture for Isaac. She could also use it as a way to let him know her, comfort her, and share in return his own regrets so that they might move forward with a better appreciation of what each had sacrificed to share the particular life that they had led together. She could hold Isaac fully responsible for the disappointments in that life or reckon with her own choices along the way. Finally, she could enter into a dialogue certain of the outcome or open to the possibility that, through it, she might actually discover something new about a man she had lived and worked with for decades.

Curiosity

Can genuine curiosity, so vital to the experience of longing and unfolding love and movement toward the beloved, really exist in a close relationship that has endured for fifty years? Or must long-married couples make do with comfort, familiarity, and shared history? It is a false dichotomy, although many couples fall into the trap of presuming to know each other so well that their capacity for discovery and surprise withers away. The ongoing ebb and flow of closeness creates stretches of separate experience and perspective for each spouse that can never be known by the other who does not look and listen with renewed curiosity. Lacking curiosity, without regularly trying to "refind" the other who is no longer quite as close as before, the cycles of ebb and flow settle into a quiet drift apart, masked by a surface of comfort, familiarity, and shared history.

In *Elegy for Iris*, John Bayley's memoir of his long marriage to the novelist and philosopher Iris Murdoch, he writes: "Inside marriage, one ceases to be observant because observation has become so automatic, its object at once absorbing and taken for granted."[17]

He is recounting the onset of his wife's Alzheimer's disease and how very hard it is to notice gradual change in someone whom you are certain you know perfectly well already. He does not depict inattention from diminished love for his wife, but simply from lovingly taking her "for granted." The same blindness through familiarity can happen with less tragic changes, even happy ones. It is so easy to miss the new that is hidden in the familiar.

Bayley tells of an earlier time when he and Murdoch were each writing and sharing their thoughts, a time that he loved:

We had already got to the stage of a relationship which Tolstoy writes about in *War and Peace*, where Pierre and Natasha, as husband and wife, understand each other and grasp each other's viewpoint without having to make sense or needing to be coherent.[18]

It is a wonderfully romantic epiphany, one that we hope all couples can experience in times of joyous closeness, yet it is a dangerous ideal. As therapists, we regularly see couples who are certain that they each "grasp each other's viewpoint" without having to attend precisely to what the other is actually saying—and get it dead wrong. Discovering the precious details of what the one we love thinks and feels and values is not only the exciting mission of new love. It is a basic maintenance routine that is essential if we are to continue to know the person we are with. In the process, we also restore a sense of freshness to familiar love.

The wider social circumstances that most older couples find themselves in, however, create particular obstacles to ongoing curiosity about each other. Age-related losses of friends and relatives compound the loss of coworkers through retirement and progressively deprive a couple of any separateness in their social worlds. Age-related limitations on activity and mobility can progressively deprive older couples of their separate interests and projects outside the marriage. Two overlapping worlds can then collapse into a single relentlessly shared routine. There is nothing to report to each other, no new experiences that have not already been shared, no enlivening gossip that the other does not know, nothing to be curious about except the other's pure thoughts and feelings. Like it or not, these are not ordinarily interesting enough to sustain another's curiosity over extended periods of time without the "props" of external events and other people, without new stories to tell. In an earlier chapter, we wrote of the natural rhythm over the workweek: attention shifts from our partner to work-related concerns and back again over the weekend. That rhythm not only makes the work of reconnecting necessary; it makes the process of reconnecting more interesting because the other has new stories to tell and has been changed, at least a little, by them. We approach each other just a bit uncertain about what we will find. It awakens curiosity and maybe even a touch of anxiety. At its best, it enlivens us and the relationship.

The malaise that often develops in couples who are deprived of this rhythm indicates that the ebb and flow of closeness is not just inevitable but sustaining. To best harness its sustaining power in the later years of marriage, a couple needs to recognize the importance of maintaining some separateness in their activities and experiences, enough time for distance so that they do not lose the revitalizing pleasure of reconnecting. To return to the Altmans, it might not be a bad thing if Rebecca took some art classes while Isaac continued to spend a few hours a week in the lab. Rather than setting them on separate trajectories, it might make them each more interesting to the other and make them look forward to coming together again after their separate pursuits, but only if they each carry their separate experiences back to the other to share.

In Sickness and in Health

Not all couples can follow this recommendation, however. Sometimes the pressures of illness and infirmity are just too much. The eighteenth-century English poet William Cowper expresses our collective hope:

> And still to love, though prest with ill,
> In wintry age to feel no chill,
> With me is to be lovely still, My Mary!

Still, we must give a hard and realistic look at these unwanted but reliable intruders during the later years of marriage. John Bayley's descriptions of the encroachment of Alzheimer's disease on his marriage with Iris Murdoch is a good place to start. He is able "still to love," but the nature of their bond is reworked by the slipping away of memory, by the burdens and incessant togetherness of caretaking, by the peculiar mix of an unbridgeable gulf and an intense closeness. His words evoke a sense of deep tenderness and of horror.

Once I was outside her, a reality quite separate from herself, her mind, her powers of being and creating. Not now.

Now I feel us fused together. It appalls me sometimes but it also seems comforting and reassuring and normal. . . . Every day we move closer and closer together.[19]

A few pages later, he adds: "I need our closeness now as much as Iris does, but I don't feel I need to cherish it. It has simply arrived, like Alzheimer's."[20]

This newfound closeness, arising from Murdoch's affliction and Bayley's response to it, is just the opposite of what he once cherished most about their marriage—the experience of being deeply involved with another person who must be approached over and over again with curiosity and wonder, the mix of movement apart and movement together that we have called ebb and flow. Here is his description of their early times together:

Already we were beginning that strange and beneficent process in marriage by which a couple can, in the words of A. D. Hope, the Australian poet, "move closer and closer apart." The apartness is a part of the closeness. . . . The solitude I have enjoyed in marriage and, I think, Iris, too, is a little like having a walk by oneself and knowing that tomorrow, or soon, one will be sharing it with the other, or, equally perhaps, again having it alone . . . [21]

So married life began. And the joys of solitude. No contradiction was involved. The one went perfectly with the other. To feel oneself held and cherished and accompanied, and yet to be alone.[22]

Out of their closeness, Bayley longs to re-create the distance that permits curiosity and renewed movement toward one another. He even imagines a wondrous distance where, most likely, none exists:

There are so many doubts and illusions and concealments in any close relationship. . . . Iris's tears sometimes seem to signify a whole inner world which she is determined to keep from me and shield me from. . . . The illusion of such an inner world still there—if it is an illusion—can't help haunting me from time to time. There are moments when I almost welcome it. Iris has always had—must have had—so vast and rich and complex an inner world, which it used to give me immense pleasure *not* to know anything about. Like looking at a map of South America as a child and wondering about the sources of the Amazon, and what unknown cities might be hidden there in the jungle.[23]

The cycles of curiosity and knowing have come to a final end, but there remains an emotional ebb and flow:

> Violent irritation possesses me and I shout out before I can stop myself, "Don't keep asking me when we are going!" . . .
> Now her face just crumples into tears. I hasten to comfort her, and she always responds to comfort. We kiss and embrace now much more than we used to.[24]

This quintessentially intellectual couple, beset by an illness that devastates the mind, must still find ways to reconnect. They do so through the simple medium of loving touch, which remains as important in old age as any other phase of life.

If touch, both sexual and nonsexual, is forgotten in an aging marriage, one of the most powerful antidotes to tidal drift is lost. Much is written these days about sexual activity and aging; much of what is written is intended to dispel the "myth" that sexual activity and pleasure must diminish with age. Although most studies have found that sexual interest and activity decrease with age, there are good reasons to believe that at least some of the decrease reflects differences in sexual behavior and expectations across generations. Culture plays an important role as well. Studies in Western societies regularly find that older individuals are seen as less sexually competent not only by their juniors but by themselves. By contrast, in preindustrial and traditional societies there is little age-related decline in sexuality for either men or women.[25]

Yet even when couples give up sexual activity entirely (which is "overwhelmingly" attributed by both men and woman to the health or attitudes of the man), they report other ways of establishing physical closeness: "sitting and lying close to each other, touching, and holding hands,"[26] much as Bayley describes.

We once heard a woman declare on the radio, "Old age is a curse!" Certainly the infirmities of old age can feel like a curse. So can the caretaking responsibilities that fall on the well spouse, whose wellness is often only relative. In one survey, 86 percent of individuals over sixty-five reported at least one chronic medical condition.[27] The curses of old age are terribly common curses. It is therefore encouraging (and perhaps a bit surprising) to find evidence that most chronic illnesses are not particularly damaging to the quality of marital bonds. When one member of a couple develops a major illness, there is usually no effect on marital satisfaction. Although the caregiving spouse obviously experiences considerable strain (consider Bayley's "violent irritation" over a constantly repeated question), the increased burden is not usually accompanied by an increase in negative feelings about the ill spouse.[28] In fact, some couples report a strengthening of their connection that arises from the process of one partner caring for the other.[29] In marriage, as in most relationships, the experience of being helpful to another person often leads to more affectionate feelings for the one we have helped. A quiet but powerful version of this effect is recounted by Benjamin Franklin in his *Autobiography*. Facing opposition in the General Assembly from an influential gentleman, Franklin made of him a lifelong friend not by doing him a favor but by receiving one: he asked to borrow "a certain very scarce and curious book," a request that was immediately granted.[30] At a much more visceral and intense extreme, the novelist Philip Roth (in his memoir *Patrimony*) describes a welling up of tenderness and a renewed sense of connection with his dying father while cleaning up the bathroom after his father's incontinence. The ebb and flow of closeness is tightly linked to cycles of helping and allowing oneself to be helped.

Couples may actually use health issues to renegotiate roles in more egalitarian ways. In a 1982 survey, husbands and wives were equally likely to leave their job to take care of an ill spouse. Caretaking husbands tended to take on more household tasks, whereas caretaking wives became more involved in financial matters.[31] Surveys reveal only statistical trends, however, not inevitable pathways. When Rebecca Altman developed problems with arthritis, Isaac took over nightly cooking chores, but he also began attending to the lab's finances, which had previously been Rebecca's domain. These duties, which had been a source of tension in the marriage for many years, were reworked in positive ways around demands of illness.

The positive feelings of the helper for the one who is helped depends, however, on a sense of efficacy. It requires being successful as a helper or at least being appreciated for trying. When caretaking demands are beyond the capacities of an also-aging spouse, a drift into bitterness or despair is all too easy. Elderly couples who are not embedded in a wider network of support—either through family or community resources—are vulnerable despite the most loving of marriage bonds. The caretaking resources that they can offer to each other are too easily depleted by the demands of chronic illness if there are no external resources to draw on. Returning to Philip Roth's transcendent experience while cleaning up after his father, he is careful to add, "If I have to do this every day, I may not wind up feeling quite so thrilled."[32]

The exception to the generally positive picture of caretaking spouses is Alzheimer's disease (despite John Bayley's loving account). It is the one chronic medical condition in which spouses reliably report a decrease in marital satisfaction. One study found that the decrease in satisfaction is specifically tied to the dementia-driven loss of "companionship."[33] Women are more likely than men to experience high levels of stress in caring for a spouse with dementia. Caregiving wives report more depression than caregiving husbands and were much more likely to describe deterioration in the marital relationship over the course of the illness. Caretaking wives also feel more burdened and have less tolerance for memory and behavior problems in their spouse. One study concluded that husbands were more likely to take an "instrumental approach" to daily problems—to keep trying things until something worked. Two years later in the illness, however, the gender differences had disappeared, not because the men had grown more burdened but because the women felt less burdened. Both women and men had also become more tolerant of the memory and behavior problems of their spouse, even though the problems themselves were generally worse.[34] The picture is not a cheerful one, but older spouses are likely to adjust successfully to a caretaking role in marriage when that task is imposed on them by illness.

Still, we must consider the "cohort effect." The divorce rate in couples over age sixty-five is still low, but it is definitely rising. It continues to increase even though the divorce rate for couples under age thirty-four has actually fallen.[35] There is every reason to expect that, as cohorts with high divorce rates during earlier phases of life reach old age, the divorce rate for elderly couples will continue to rise. All the data we have on successful adaptation to chronic illness and caretaking in elderly marriages is based on couples who, by and large, have viewed the covenant of marriage as a much more binding commitment than their children do. Tidal drift will continue to affect marriages in the later years. Its motion will continue to be complicated by the stresses of illness and caretaking. We currently have evidence that couples usually respond to extreme strains on a marriage with determined efforts to sustain a connection and to find new modes of reconnecting. These efforts are often successful, despite seemingly oppressive obstacles. Whether the next generation of elderly couples will make the same effort and experience the same success are questions that will be answered over time.

While we wait, we may as well give John Bayley the last word:

Looking back, I separate us with difficulty. We seem always to have been together. . . . As I work in bed early in the morning, typing on my old portable with Iris quietly asleep beside me, her presence as she is now seems as it always was, and as it always should be. I know she must once have been different, but I have no true memory of a different person.[36]

7

Covenants that Limit Drift

Marriage, Parenthood, and Other Family Obligations

If even the best relationships experience a natural ebb and flow, from short periods of a week's duration to longer periods of several years, why do some couples feel they have simply grown apart in an irreparable way while others ride the drifts over decades and feel that they have grown closer? What distinguishes couples with "drift tolerance" from those who see the drift as a painful erosion of their most deep-seated feelings of love?

Our work with couples who are struggling with uncertainties about their future suggests that those who are able to weather the ebb and flow of tidal drift typically share two characteristics. The first is an intuitive feel for this curious aspect of closeness. Most often, their "intuition" seems to be grounded in their observations of a lasting relationship between their own parents. They also know how to use the covenant aspect of their marriage vows, the simple but powerful fact of a formal and solemn commitment, as a powerful aid in changing the direction of the drift. A covenant, when taken seriously, gives each partner the right to speak up and *do* something about a developing distance rather than take it as a sign that the relationship has run its course and it is time to let go. The effort to "reel in" a partner who is drifting too far is understood (at least some of the time) as an act of love, not a betrayal of an individual's potential for growth.

This shared commitment is crucial because the "reeling in" process is not always pretty. Although many marriage self-help books imply that it can be done in a low-key, ever-so-constructive tone that negates the need for anger or argument, in real life it might take the form of a fight, a sexual encounter, a tantrum, an ultimatum, or some combination of these devices for refocusing attention. Many times the person caught up in the act of reeling in a drifting partner will not realize consciously that reconnection is the purpose behind the drama. But reconnection happens and both partners are the closer for it. Because of the reestablishment of closeness (and the security it brings), comfortable glacial drift apart sets in all over again.

Overactive Alarm Systems

The alarm system cannot be too sensitive, however, or like the din of car alarms in the city, the warning sirens themselves become intolerable. What is needed is an approach that (in another context) the psychiatrist Leston Havens calls "loose holding." Although a covenant can provide the basis for holding fast in the face of threatening disconnections, an intuitive grasp of the ebb and flow of closeness creates a flexibility in the bond so that ordinary shifts in interest and attention are not transformed into calamitous rifts. Adults who are most wedded to a blueprint of the romantic ideal, who envision a loving closeness unaffected by the passage of time, become so overwhelmed by pessimism in the face of natural drift that they cannot allow their relationship to continue. They either become shrill and demanding, driving a spouse even further away, or precipitously end a marriage that they feel certain is already doomed. Paradoxically, these dreamers' idealism does not come from having ever witnessed the love they desire. Instead, they usually have grown up with parents whose marriage seemed unsatisfactory and are terrified of following the same unhappy path. They are determined to avoid it at all costs and view any imperfection in their own relationships as confirmation of their worst fears. Only the most idealized romantic notion of love seems to offer any hope at all, so they hold fast to an ideal that can wreak havoc in a marriage. In fact, we often see a kind of hypervigilance (overattention) to the degree of distance in the partner who is most attached to the romantic ideal, with a tendency toward catastrophizing worry at the slightest sign of a shift toward greater distance.

How would this worry look in real life? We have worked with several couples in which the wife felt so dangerously excluded by her husband's hobby, be it surfing the Internet or playing the guitar, that she saw it as a sign of deep pathology. From her point of view, either her husband was weirdly disconnected from people or he had no interest in her anymore. Although the husband might put aside his hobby to spend more time with his wife, when he later returned to it after what he hoped was reassuring time together, the wife would again feel that her worst fears about his disconnection were confirmed. Without the notion of natural shifts of attention to other concerns after a phase of increasing closeness, the wife could only see the husband's pursuit of a hobby as an escape from intimacy. Frightened attempts to prove that either the husband or the marriage was fundamentally flawed, however, transformed a predictable phasic shift into a symbol of hopelessness. The alarm was sounded not as a call for ordinary readjustment but as a death knell. The only adequate response would be the husband's transformation. A temporary shift in attention simply will not do. Since most of us are extremely limited in our capacity for transformation, the husband soon began to share his wife's hopelessness about the marriage. Although sometimes a fight or a tantrum is just what a relationship needs for a renewal of closeness, the battle must be fought to preserve the relationship, not to prove that it is dead. The wife's vision of a perfect relationship was based on a heroic attempt to avoid the separateness that she had seen developing in her own parents' marriages. In our book *Overcoming Loneliness in Everyday Life*, we emphasized the importance of shared tasks and interests in sustaining a marriage. Marriages in which neither spouse has a "distance alarm" are in grave danger. The trick is to distinguish normal shifts in closeness from lives set on dangerously separate trajectories.

The Importance of the Marriage Vow

Holding that is too loose can be just as damaging to a relationship as holding that is too tight. That is where covenants become important. Marriage vows—"to have and to hold from this day forward, for better, for worse, for richer, for poorer, in sickness and health, to love and to cherish till death do us part"—create a right to complain and seek restorative action if "having and holding" has disappeared from the relationship because of drift. Even the language of the classic wedding vow, with its unforgettable dialectic rhythm detailing the ups and downs of feeling and circumstance ("for better for worse, for richer for poorer, . . . ") implies a movement back and forth between poles that need to be mastered in all marriages. The absence of such a vow leaves each partner wondering, "So how much can he/she stand before he/she kicks me out?"

A formal promise makes the renewal of closeness an explicit obligation for both parties, whether external circumstances or internal feelings are causing a drift apart. It counters the lure of a lazy pessimism, of demoralized but tempting statements such as "What's the use?" A promise frames an obligation that helps adhere the relationship in the face of the constant entropylike drag toward greater distance that often occurs after the early stages in even the best of relationships. Lacking an overt promise, it is much harder for a couple to weather the changes that happen in a close relationship over time. If one person notices the other emotionally wandering, there is no mutual agreement to do something about it in order to prolong the relationship. Drift is far more threatening; it is seen as foreshadowing an exit rather than an effort at renewal.

We suggest that the current trend toward living together without marriage creates problems for couples and their children in forming long-lasting relationships. Many modern couples profess that they do not need the reassurance of a mere "piece of paper" to support their love, but they confuse issues of bureaucracy with the powerful effects that a ritual of public commitment to each other will have on their own perception and behavior. The formal promise matters immensely for withstanding the inevitable ebbs and flows in their experience of closeness over years.

Some people have argued that marriage vows only lead to a chronic state of taking and being taken "for granted" and thus should be avoided on that basis. Edmund Morris, a friend of ours who never married his partner Carol, once remarked that during a marriage to another woman, he and his wife grew blasé and bored with each other. He purposely decided never to marry again because he blamed the boredom on the marriage contract. He strongly believes that he and Carol continue to be very much in love with each other after fifteen years together because the lack of a marriage contract keeps both of them "on their toes." On the other hand, insecurity is not the only reason to make an effort. A marriage contract is no more an impediment to a couple's ongoing fascination with each other than tenure is an inevitable obstruction to a professor's scholarly accomplishment. A position that offers security can act as a spur to creativity, not only an opportunity to take advantage of a sinecure. Besides, with divorce so common, no couple can realistically hope that a marriage contract gives them license to stop trying to make their lives together interesting.

Ironically, it is liberating to have a vow of commitment that lets us sit tight even when the intensity of the relationship waxes and wanes over time. We need not pack up our belongings every time we notice increasing distance in a relationship because we have promised to find ways to renew our closeness. We need not sink all of our creative energy into the perpetual question of whether we should go or stay. But the effort that this obligation requires is very real—we need to work (and play) to combat that entropylike force we call the drift. Neither man nor woman is exempt from fighting the trend toward increasing distance if it has become bothersome to the other. In the best of circumstances, each partner will experience the distance as worrisome at approximately the same time. More often, as we discussed in Chapter 3, the woman may find a particular state of conversational disconnection (and therefore distance) worrisome when the man thinks it is just right. Conversely, the woman may feel a certain amount of sexual distance quite comfortable while the man perceives it as sexually depriving. How can couples cope with their different levels of distance tolerance?

The Advantages of Multiple Alarm Systems

We think couples need to remember that there are advantages to each partner's alarm system. Evolutionary psychologists suggest that men's lower threshold for sexual arousal compared to women's make it likely that they will impregnate a woman or women more often, thus ensuring the survival of their sperm. They also believe that women's greater ability to vigilantly protect their offspring through close observation of emotions and careful monitoring of relationships make it more likely that her offspring will survive. Even though these evolutionary views might favor consecutive, monogamous relationships producing more healthy offspring, biological differences can be harnessed to prolong the quality and length of marriages. We simply must recognize that each offers different means for renewing closeness. Sexual intercourse often creates a sense of rejuvenation, relaxation, and intimacy as its by-product. A frank conversation about feelings can similarly enhance a sense of intimacy. Couples may argue about which mode of connection should be used on a given night, but these evolutionary differences can be transformed to renew closeness if each partner respects the other's way of signaling that an increasing distance is becoming dangerous. The more typical response of feeling crowded by the other's desires does not allow our separate alarm systems to be properly valued as a stroke of evolutionary luck that protects our most intimate relationships with backup alarm systems, just the kind of redundancy that safety engineers would want to see.

Let us repeat the points of our argument. First, there is a natural ebb and flow in all human relationships, including those of strong romantic love. Marriage vows are helpful to all long-term monogamous relationships because they provide a framework in which each partner can insist on the right to "reel the other partner in" when the drift seems too great. Men and women whose parents had strong marriages have a better intuitive sense for this phenomenon because they have often watched it firsthand during the formative years of early life. Children whose parents' marriage did not work well find it easy to catastrophize the ebb and flow that goes on in all healthy relationships. The ordinary ebb and flow may then be misunderstood as the permanent departure of romantic love from a marriage and lead to the shattering of a relationship that could have lasted and deepened over time. As more children of divorced parents reach marriageable age, they need to be taught the natural course of healthy, long-term relationships and the role that covenants can play in strengthening them to prevent an ongoing cycle of unnecessary divorce.

Tidal Patterns in Raising Children

The ebb-and-flow principle in human relationships seems much more palatable and even commonsensical to most people when they are raising children. It makes sense precisely because of the clear though unwritten covenant that binds parents to their offspring. Couples who misunderstand drift in their marriage can often grasp it much more accurately in their relationship with their children and either work to remedy it or simply leave it be, depending on the child's developmental stage. Most parents do not assume their child has left forever if at seven she seems to prefer playing at a friend's house down the street. We usually think that mothers or fathers who feel too hurt by a child's preference for the other house need guidance from friends, relatives or professionals to re-establish a connection with the child without imposing their own insecurities on the child's developing curiosity about the outside world.

From the earliest years, toddlers take off in exploratory circles after "refueling" at their mother's knee. Therefore, we are not surprised by the pattern of distancing followed by renewed closeness in a child's normal development. Parents and children expect to grow apart as children mature and get ready to leave the nest. But in this long process, there are thousands of mini-leavetakings and returnings as parents and children regulate the intensity of attachment they need or can stand at any particular moment. As children go through the attaching and detaching process in toddlerhood, they get ready for the greater independence of school. As they progress through elementary school, their values about obligation toward family members may become conscious and codified. Frequently, the hormonal storms of puberty then blow the code into a new form to fit the child's increasing sexual viability.

Unwritten Covenants with Children

When the importance of family is clear to a child through the elementary school years, then a parallel structure to the covenant of marriage is created between the child and parents. The parents, however, need to shore up their side of the covenant by practicing their belief in the cohesion and loyalty of the family in everyday life. Although the covenant might not be spelled out, the notion that "you can count on your family" is there for many children in the daily atmosphere of their home. It allows children to feel that, even if they are locked in battle with their parents, there is a mutual obligation and promise of loyalty that will carry them through difficult times.

Yet some families are much more "successful" than others at remaining a family even after the children grow up. Some ethnic groups such as Asians, Italians, or Jews are often considered particularly good at emphasizing "family values" and their upward mobility in American society is regularly attributed to this emphasis. How do so-called successful families weather the storms of adolescence and the vicissitudes of long-distance relationships after adolescents have left home better than others? What, if anything, does this sturdiness of family have to do with covenants similar to those of marriage?

The importance of loyalty and connection to family can be instilled in children on a daily and weekly basis like the air they breathe and the food they chew. It becomes a sacred notion much like marriage vows or a belief in God. The advantage of this lesson, demonstrated by the words and behavior of parents, is that children will grow up to make this invisible covenant their own. Should a family rift occur when they are grown and living at a distance, then, they will feel as much of an obligation to heal and restore meaningful connection as their parents. It is this sense of *mutual* obligation between children and parents that makes certain family ties more sturdy than when the obligation to family is left much more vague or one-sided.

The Pantals are a family with adult children who have a clear sense of responsibility to keep the family close. Anita and Dal immigrated to this country from India when their two children, Rondala and Vikram, were twelve and fourteen years old, respectively. The parents had a hard time getting established in Milwaukee. Although Dal eventually was successful as a software programmer, the family's outsider status during the early years led them to grow extremely close, almost "cocooned." Much later, when the children were adults (ages twenty-four and twenty-six) and living independently in Boston, their father became depressed and aloof. He began to let his wife do all the talking on the phone, which was not at all like him. When Rondala and Vikram came to visit, Dal was no longer his usual passionate self and his children felt they were losing touch with him. A few months later, Dal suggested over the phone that both children come to a resort on Lake Michigan for a long weekend with their parents. He offered them short notice—less than a week's lead time. They both decided to go, despite the inconvenience. As Rondala put it, "Our family has been through so much together and stayed so close. We have to try to do our part to reconnect with Dad whenever he's ready, whether it's easy or not."

Strengthening Family Ties During Separations

One can make a good argument in favor of spelling out the following for adolescents who are about to leave home. First, *rifts are much more likely to occur at long distance*, where day-to-day contact can no longer smooth ruffled feathers and hurt feelings. Second, *adolescents who have departed have an equal responsibility in healing rifts*. Of course, this will only "take" if the ground has been prepared beforehand through years of demonstrating how loyalty and making up after fights actually works.

Over recent years, we have noticed in many families an exaggeration of the storms of adolescence that lead well-educated and well-intentioned parents to act as if it is quite normal for an adolescent to withdraw completely from family obligations. For example, we have frequently heard the following comments in discussions with mothers or fathers. "Of course, we didn't get any letters when he went away for overnight camp. After all, he's a teenager now." Or, "We went on vacation for a week, but of course she won't come with us any more now that she's an adolescent." Or, "He's gone now. Even though he's not leaving for college for six months, we can't get him to a family meal because he's withdrawing from the family. You know these teenagers." These conversations imply a mutual understanding between family members that things are just the way they should be and parents should simply hold hands as they get ready for the empty nest that is the destiny of an American family. These conversations leave unacknowledged the parents' wish to be done with child rearing and its inevitable laundries, meal preparation, and worry that have worn out so many working parents that they yearn to be done with it. But most adolescents surely get the message that their withdrawal is both right and expected. The statistics on increasing anger and depression among adolescents should not surprise us so much. One terrible lesson from the school killings in Columbine, Colorado, is that adolescents can live comfortably at home and still be hopelessly disconnected from their seemingly well-meaning parents.

Effects of Staying Connected with Children

Recently, a large government-sponsored study of adolescent health appeared in the *Journal of the American Medical Association*. It concluded that adolescents

> who reported a connectedness to their parents were less likely to engage in risky behavior such as cigarette, alcohol, marijuana use, violent behavior, suicide and sexual activity. These young people felt close to their parents, felt their parents cared about them and were satisfied with their family relationships. To a lesser extent, adolescents were also protected from risky behaviors by their parents being present at key times during the day.[1]

This study affirms the idea that connectedness even in the separating adolescent is an asset for survival and a sense of well-being.

But "connectedness" and the covert covenant between parents and children mean different things in different cultures. For example, in current American culture, nurturing connectedness in teenagers means giving up an honored, though relatively recent tradition, namely, that an eighteen-year-old child goes out on his or her own, becomes self-supporting, and never really comes home again. This expectation is not conducive to family connectedness since it requires an abrupt separation at a rather arbitrary time. When parents or children hold this idea, they work to transform the natural ebb-and-flow pattern in family relationships to one that simply ebbs in preparation for the massive change. We should not be surprised when reckless, devil-may-care behavior shows up in adolescents who react to the impending loss. At present, we are in a time of cultural transition in which it is becoming far less stigmatized (and less associated with old-country ways) for a young adult to live at home for economic reasons. This model of living with family as an adult, so common in Western European countries, may be a better model for sustaining connections between grown children and parents, although it requires some version of the concept of "loose holding" to avoid a sense of constriction and stifled development.

In relationships between parents and young children, parents set the example as well as the tone. If parents are disengaged from their children's lives, pretty soon the children feel neglected and act in a way that may be unconsciously designed to get the parents reconnected but often increases the estrangement. In *Beyond the Classroom: Why School Reform Has Failed and What Parents Need to Do*, Lawrence Steinberg has examined data from surveys in California and Wisconsin high schools.[2] He found that one-quarter of parents were basically passive, preoccupied or downright negligent. Only a third of students reported having daily conversations with their parents and half of the parents said they did not know who their children's friends were or what their children did after school. Not surprisingly, the children of parents who were most out of touch were the ones who engaged in the most risky behaviors including drugs, alcohol, and sex.

The vague, unspecified nature of the covenant in many families, especially during a time of cultural change, is leading to many social problems. Women and men are expected to work full time and single parents are often supporting families alone. Thus, we find less social pressure for parents to stay connected with children. Instead, we have come to expect just the opposite: "How can you expect him to talk to his mother and father? He's a *teenager*, after all." In our culture, we anticipate the worst from our adolescent children without noticing the part played by our own low expectations.

The successful immigrant groups who have achieved the American dream in one or two generations have spelled out most clearly the emphasis on family connectedness. Usually such families have the determined underdog feeling, "It's us against them and we have to help each other as much as possible." In these families, we find mothers who drive to school in the middle of the day to bring a child's forgotten homework rather than "letting him learn from his mistakes," as more established families might do. This philosophy results in a supportive group and a cheering section for each young person who is preparing to go out in the world. If one of them earns a superlative education at an elite college, the family (including the child) feels that they have triumphed as a whole. The ebb and flow of relationships is allowed, but only with the understanding that children stay connected even after they achieve success. Unfortunately, if the young people "jump class" through their elite education, connectedness becomes awkward and embarrassing. Parents can feel inferior to their children and children can feel ashamed of their parents. Even a strong emphasis on "family values" cannot always overcome this metamorphosis caused by the achievement of the American dream in a culture that often equates success with standing apart.

Similarly, when the parents have achieved a lifestyle much more "comfortable" (usually a euphemism for lavish) than that of their children and are unwilling to share their wealth, the lack of ease between generations can be equally disconcerting. Severe envy becomes a barrier to connection because a renewal of closeness serves as a reminder of the inequalities of status or material wealth. If connectedness between parents and grown-up children is to be a satisfying reality, parents must try to ensure that their children will be as successful as they have been in the world. This may mean personal sacrifice so that their children's education will be the equivalent of their own. Given shifting economic expectations in this country, there may need to be a previously unnecessary section to the unwritten covenant between parents and children: we will stay connected as a family and work hard to ensure that the younger members have as good a chance at happiness and material success as the older members.

Most people describe what is meant by "family values" as an unspoken vow to stay loyal and remain caring in their feelings and actions to their nuclear family (and to extended family members when these values are strongest). If these ideas are spelled out in day-to-day discussions and activities of child rearing, they are likely to have far-reaching effects. We may never wish to have a piece of paper like a marriage contract that defines obligations between parents and children. The clearer we are on the implicitly covenanted nature of parenthood, however, the better our children are likely to turn out . . . and the more likely they are to take the covenant seriously when they have children of their own.

Children "separate" from their parents through the widening circles of independence that occur at each stage of development. When a covenant or sacred value has been placed on family connections, the final result is a sense of autonomy and identity that does not depend on complete separateness, a reworking rather than a severing of bonds. The same flexible and loving tenacity can then be used as tool to deal with similar cycles of closeness and distance in the lasting relationships of their adulthood, including romance and marriage.

8

From Casanova to Canute
Character Types that Fight the Tides

A love suspended in time with no beginning or end.
Lydia Flem
Casanova: The Man Who Really Loved Women

The following words were spoken by a remarkably accomplished man of fifty, well spoken, well read, and successful in a range of ventures, including scholarship and business.

> With each new relationship, it's not just the excitement of the sex, as good as that is. It's a whole new circle of friends, a new set of interests, a new kind of music to listen to, even new books to read. . . . It's the only time I don't feel that something is missing from me, that a part of me is absent.

In his love life, Joseph Kim might be described as unusually successful or deeply flawed. It all depends on the definition of success. Twice married and twice divorced, he has taken as lovers an ongoing procession of beautiful women. He can narrate his life as a story of exuberant and triumphant sexuality that inspires envy and applause. He can also tell it as a story of driven and destructive sexuality that elicits prescriptions for Prozac and psychotherapy. Speaking with him, it quickly becomes clear that he sees both versions as bewilderingly divergent truths about himself.

His uncertainty is shared by the surrounding society. If someone is called a Casanova or a Don Juan, we must first know the speaker and the context to decide if it's a tribute or a condemnation. Joseph Kim has been knowingly congratulated and roundly condemned. That same ambivalence was manifest throughout the Clinton sex scandals, not just in the argument but even more dramatically in the counterpoint between a moral-political debate and an endless series of leering jokes that together formed the warp and woof of public and private discourse. As the whole country knows by now, psychiatrists and psychologists have a wide range of labels and theories to explain "pathologies" of sexuality and personal attachment. We can focus on the importance of inherited biology, on the specifics of an individual's developmental path to adulthood, on the sociopolitical dimensions of gender and power. Each perspective has something to offer Joseph as he thinks about whether he wants to change his life and whether he can. An understanding of tidal drift in relationships will also be essential to him—his words already reach in that direction. He represents one of several character types who display either an inability or unwillingness to tolerate the natural drifts in a lasting relationship. In this chapter, we move from the ordinary difficulties in riding out the ebbs and flows of close relationships to the extraordinary difficulties that particular characters encounter around issues of closeness, change, and time. We will bracket these character types with two individuals, historical but mythologized, who symbolize opposite extreme responses to a universal uneasiness with the relentless flow of time: Casanova, whose name has come to represent ceaseless, exuberant movement from one fresh seduction to the next, and Canute, the eleventh-century English king who commanded the tides to stop.

Attachment Theory and Adult Love

Attachment theory is an approach to human development pioneered by the British psychiatrist John Bowlby.[1] He started with a simple behavioral observation: infants and young children who are separated from their mother (or more generally, their primary caretaker) show a predictable series of emotional responses over time. First comes protest—

crying, searching, refusing comfort from unwanted substitutes. Then despair—a passive collapse, a giving up, a look of sadness. Finally, if the separation goes on long enough, there is a stage of detachment in which the mother, when she finally returns, is avoided or ignored. The first two stages are also seen in nonhuman primates.[2] Bowlby viewed attachment (or "affectional bonding") as a complex behavioral system that is essential to the survival of both individual and species. It serves to maintain a reasonable degree of physical closeness between a vulnerable child and his primary caregiver. Attachment behavior functions as a spring, allowing a degree of freedom but creating an increasing tension that pulls mother and infant toward each other when the separation is too great. The result is oscillation around a set point of comfort, the human version of physics' simple harmonic motion—the movement of two masses attached by a spring.

This movement is commonly observed in toddlers, who toddle off happily to explore the world, secure that mother is there but periodically return to her for "refueling." If the return is blocked, joyful exploration ceases and Bowlby's sequence of reactions to loss take over. At an earlier age and on a more subtle scale, infants actively modulate the intensity of engagement with caregivers by alternately making eye contact and then averting their gaze, creating and controlling cycles of closeness and distance.[3] The near-universal game of peek-a-boo shows how this cycle can be transformed into an experience of gaiety and laughter for an infant. It also supports a statement of Bowlby's that is deeply connected to the process of ebb and flow: "The unchallenged maintenance of a bond is experienced as a source of security, and the renewal of a bond as a source of joy."[4]

In the 1970s, infant researcher Mary Ainsworth developed a strategy to study systematically the quality of an infant's attachment to its mother.[5] A mother, a young child, and an observer sit together in a small room. At a certain moment, the mother leaves the room, leaving behind an object closely associated with her, like a pocketbook. The observer records the child's responses to the mother's absence and her subsequent return. Ainsworth evocatively titled her work "A Psychological Study of the Strange Situation." Her group identified three types of attachment: secure, anxious/ambivalent, and avoidant. Although each type is characterized by detailed behavioral observations, essentially each style of attachment means just what its name suggests. The "strange situation test" has become a basic tool of child development researchers.

Attachment theory gracefully straddles the usual division between biology and psychology. Attachment behavior must clearly be inherent to the organism, molded by both the infant and mother's inborn temperaments, yet also shaped in an ongoing way by each participant's accumulating experience with the other. It is reasonable to wonder if the behavioral pattern that is so basic to our survival continues to shape "affectional bonds" throughout the life cycle, in an obviously complex interaction with two other behavioral systems defined by Bowlby and Ainsworth—caregiving and mating. Three psychologists, Phillip Shaver, Cindy Hazan, and Donna Bradshaw, have considered this question. They developed a theory of love as attachment behavior and attempted to extend Ainsworth's categories of secure, anxious/ambivalent, and avoidant styles of attachment to adult patterns of romantic love.[6] Their work is as yet inconclusive, particularly the attempt to establish continuity between infant and adult attachment styles. They have, however, studied two groups with a "Love Quiz" (twelve hundred people responded to it when it appeared in the *Rocky Mountain News;* they then administered it to over one hundred university students). A majority of the respondents (56 percent of each group) could be characterized as secure in their approach to love, approximately one quarter were avoidant, and the remainder (about 20 percent) were anxious/ambivalent.

Although attachment theory may seem to have led us away from the sexier attachments of a Casanova or a Don Juan, we can now loop back to those gentlemen by way of the following conclusions from the Love Quiz:

> Secure lovers more often said that romantic feelings wax and wane but at times reach the intensity experienced at the start of the relationship, and that in some relationships romantic love never fades. Avoidant lovers said that the kind of head-over-heels romantic love depicted in novels and movies doesn't exist in real life, that romantic love rarely

lasts, and that it is rare to find a person one can *really* fall in love with. Anxious/ambivalent respondents claimed it is easy to fall in love and said that they frequently feel themselves beginning to do so, although (like the avoidant lovers) they rarely find what they would call "real" love.[7]

In other words, secure lovers are most likely to experience (or more accurately to *notice*) the phenomenon of ebb and flow in their romantic feelings.

There is actually a complex relationship between noticing ebb and flow and experiencing it. Individuals who have already noticed it are also much more likely to experience it—they stick around when feelings ebb long enough to find that they can start to flow again. Those who lack that confidence are already long gone. The result is that we are most likely to keep discovering the "truth" about love that we already believe. Infants in the "strange situation" have no choice but to wait and see if their mother returns. Adults in the romantic equivalent of the strange situation have more options—they are mobile. Those who lack confidence in the return of a lover or, more important, in the return of love will usually not wait passively to have their worst fears confirmed. They seek the renewed hope of a freshly unfolding love; they try to freeze time and embalm the love they have; or they withdraw from love altogether. It is among these "insecure" lovers that we must seek our Casanovas and our Canutes.

Let us return to Joseph Kim's opening words. He is not just describing a one-dimensional sexual fling. He is conjuring up a whole new life, a rebirth that is as much intellectual as sensual. Later on, he will say, "After a year with a woman, it's not that I'm disappointed in the other person or in myself. It's just that I know her and that's all." In previous chapters, we discussed the desire for novelty as an element in all relationships and as a powerfully driving force in the lives of particular individuals. We could place Joseph in the latter camp and leave it at that. After all, temperamental differences in response to novel stimuli are among the most stable characteristics of infants and children. Some people simply like adventure and surprise more than others. Joseph enjoys throwing himself into new work situations with almost as much enthusiasm as new relationships. Yet something else seems to be going on in individuals who must continually jettison each attained intimacy in search of the next novel one. The "something else" is a profound uneasiness at the first hint of a drift apart that sends them off in a desperate quest for a new love that feels like it is unfolding rather than dying. Joseph's "and that's all" hints sadly at the inevitable waning of intensity after a year with a woman and the conviction that it will never return. It is the adult version of an infant sitting in a room with a memento of its mother but no confidence that she will ever return or, if she does, that she will arrive too late to restore comfort and joy to his world. It is a picture of relational drift not as a natural process of ebb and flow but a movement straight toward a high cliff. The Casanovas of the world respond to this picture by fleeing and seeking a new love to lie with in a springtime field far from the cliff's edge. Over and over again.

Casanova

What creates a Casanova—someone who must perpetually seek rebirth in a new relationship to ward off the feeling that love is irretrievably dying? Literary and folk traditions, along with some recent evolutionary psychologists (as we discussed in Chapter 3), expect a Casanova to be a man, but it is clearly time to include women. It may be hard to imagine an eighteenth-century woman writing memoirs that read like Giacomo Casanova's *Story of My Life*, a saga of joyful love and genuine enthusiasm for a series of 122 women, but it is fairly easy to imagine a late twentieth-century version in a woman's hand. The dual liberations of effective contraception and economic independence now make it safer for women who dread relational drift to respond by moving on rather than by holding tight. The number of young men who feel "seduced and abandoned" by young women has clearly increased over the last two decades. Is a female icon who can be placed alongside Casanova about to emerge from our culture? The seductive spy Mata Hari won't do, since espionage rather than pleasure was her goal. Actress Elizabeth Taylor functions as a kind of transitional figure, who seeks renewal not in unencumbered affairs but in a seemingly endless series of traditional marriages. Pop star Madonna, in some of her incarnations, seems to celebrate herself as a female Casanova carefully designed for an age that treasures visual images more than the written word. Even her self-consciousness is a bit Casanova-like. After all, we would not know his name if he had not written a twelve-volume history of his life.

Perhaps the most fitting female parallel for the moment is the writer Anäis Nin. Her seven volumes of published diary were daring enough on their own to create around the life of this modern woman the same mix of literary and sexual fascination that is attached to Casanova's memoirs. After the death of Nin's husband in 1986, two more "unexpurgated" volumes then increased to the hundreds the number of her affairs with major literary figures and added an adult episode of incest with her father. The result has been lingering questions about the boundaries between historical truth, creative imagination, and self-promoting myth-making in her writings, questions that surround Casanova as well. Both writers manage to portray an exuberant intensity in their sensual pursuits. Both writers also communicate a wild roller-coaster quality in their lives, with rapid alternation between bliss and suffering. Moments of sexual and literary triumphs were for each of them the most reliable antidotes to despair.

We must therefore discard gender alone as a necessary cause in creating a Casanova. Inborn temperament must certainly still play a role, however, whether directly through the strength of sexual drives or indirectly through the degree of attraction to novelty and change. Early childhood experiences with parents are also always included when "the usual suspects" are rounded up. Shaver, Hazan, and Bradshaw believe that an individual's attachment style is relatively stable over time. Seeking evidence for this hypothesis, they found that adults' attachment styles correlated with their descriptions of how each parent behaved toward them in childhood.[8] Although memories of childhood are subject to complicated distortions, the life of the real Casanova, particularly as told by the Belgian psychoanalyst Lydia Flem in her recent biography *Casanova: The Man Who Really Loved Women*, seems to support the researchers' suspicions. Giacomo Casanova emerges as a breathtakingly talented and accomplished individual whose life was powerfully shaped by two early relationships—with his mother and with death.

"Anxiously attached" is a phrase that seems to apply to his relationship with his mother, but Flem's descriptions flesh out the abstraction by evoking a mixture of hope and terror. Casanova writes of a moment when, as a boy of eleven, he was summoned to see his mother before she set off on her next journey and briefly won her admiration with his wit and intelligence. Flem continues:

> In his Bohemian retreat, Casanova recalls his mother's look of surprise and pride. As beautiful as daylight, is the way she seemed to his childish eyes. Beautiful and distant. For a fleeting moment he had succeeded in capturing the attention of this inaccessible mother who had turned away from him right after his birth. For a fleeting moment he had felt happy under her gaze.[9]

He has captured her gaze and while he is in it, he is fully alive and joyful. But he has no hope of holding it, no hope that, in the natural cycle of things, his mother's gaze once averted will return to him again. There is no tidal rhythm of connection, only a moment of joyful capture, which is repeated again and again through his life. And there is no waiting around for the inevitable moment in which a woman's gaze is at last averted from him. (Here is a further partial parallel to Anaïs Nin. Like Casanova, she had a charming, seductive, and abandoning parent of the opposite sex. She was, however, physically and perhaps sexually abused in her childhood, which is one way that "typical" stories for men and women may diverge. The divergence may decrease in the future. Although over the last two decades, seductive fathers have been relabeled as abusers, the notion that a boy is lucky to be "initiated" into sexual experience by a worldly, beautiful mother lingers, as it does in Louis Malle's movie of loving incest *Murmur of the Heart.*)

Casanova was expected to die in early childhood; incessant nosebleeds subsided only after a magical ceremony arranged by his grandmother. Death was a real presence early on, although it was one that could be thwarted through love and cleverness. But to thwart death, one must repudiate the passage of time. Again quoting Flem:

"Travel becomes a way of avoiding duration. Casanova journeys in space in order to escape time. . . . In every new place, he has hopes of a fresh start, sometimes even of rebirth."[10]

We are reminded again of Joseph Kim's comments. The best way to deny death is to be reborn, to find new life in a fresh love and the whole new world that surrounds it. Yet this strategy has its limits. Flem continues: "However, with the onset of age, the adventurer is losing his stamina and fortune becomes miserly. . . . It becomes harder and harder to preserve freedom and lightness intact, and repeatedly to jettison the past."[11] Casanova's final answer (according to Flem) is to take pen in hand and bring about one last (and lasting) rebirth through literature. To be a genuine Casanova, it helps to be exceptionally talented.

But what of more ordinary Casanovas? The ones that we have known or worked with have not all been threatened by a premature death in their childhood. Yet they too seem to wish to step out of ordinary time and to escape from any sense of "duration" in relationships. Many of them are also haunted by a specter of death from their childhood, not physical death but relational death that they witnessed in their parents' marriage and fear in their own. Often they describe (as Joseph does) a stable but affectionless marriage between their parents, one marked by emotional distance or perhaps subtle contempt. Again, remember that children's memories of their parents' relationships may be inaccurate; moments of tenderness may take place outside the child's view or remain unseen by a child who does not wish to see them. Nevertheless, these memories accurately represent a child's lasting *picture* of closeness between adults. Parental divorce tends to make children wary of emotional commitment, but memories of a joyless parental marriage can create a dread of a death-in-relationship that stretches grimly through time. For these individuals, the ebbing of first passions does not carry the threat of a shattered relationship, which at least offers the hope of better passions to follow. The danger is a living death in which the tide never turns, where time itself is oppressive, and the only antidote is perpetual rebirth through a series of new loves plucked at the height of their intensity and discarded before they begin to fade.

Frank MacPhearson is another fifty-year-old man who rejoices in the freshness of sexual discovery with new partners, only occasionally pausing in his explorations out of concern for his tense but (for the moment) enduring marriage. Frank happily explains that, for him, it is often "just" about sex. Sex is fraught with meaning, however, the center of an impassioned and well-articulated political and philosophical view of the world. Sex is both pleasurable and a heroic calling, as he pushes the envelope of conventional sensibilities and categories. Joseph welcomed a trial of Prozac, which decreased the intensity and persistence of sexual urges that he felt were derailing his life. (It remains unclear if this action is a direct effect of the medication on sexual function or an indirect consequence of treating an underlying chronic depression.) Frank, by contrast, recoiled with horror at the idea of pharmacologically altering something so essential to his identity and his beliefs. We can imagine a similar response from Casanova, were he offered the same choice.

Frank's parents seemed distant and unaffectionate with each other. As a teenager, he learned from his mother that his "real" father was a ballroom dance instructor with whom she had a brief but passionate affair. Throughout most of her marriage, she had no sexual contact with her solid and stable businessman husband. Therefore, Frank not only grew up in a world of insecure attachments, but his mother underlined the fragility of connections. Frank feels that women must be repeatedly seduced or a deathlike state intervenes and he becomes like his (nominal) father. More precisely, he becomes like the image of his father that he and his mother shared, a devitalized man who is at best tenuously connected to both mother and son. Despite Frank's exuberance, death hovers nearby: he has recently begun to experience vivid, intrusive images of blowing his brains out with a revolver. He connects these pictures to an emerging terror that he may finally be surrendering to a desexualized married life. Each sexual adventure briefly dispels the images and restores a sense of vitality and hope. An ebb and flow of intensity and intimacy is created by movement from one partner to the next. He sees no reason to believe that it can exist for him within a single lasting relationship. Perhaps for Frank, for now, it cannot; duration and death are too closely linked.

Canute

Although some individuals manage their mistrust of intimate relationships through constant motion, reigniting life and hope with novelty, others take the opposite approach. Once love is found, they feel their only hope is to freeze a relationship in its youth through constant vigilance against any movement or change. It is a noble effort doomed to failure. They remind us of the figure of King Canute, sitting on his throne in rising water vainly commanding the tide to stop.

There is a legend attached to Canute the Great, the eleventh-century Viking conqueror who was the first king to unite all of England. His courtiers, in their flattery and pride, had proclaimed that their king's words could control the very tides. Canute ordered his throne carried to the shoreline at low tide, sat upon it, and commanded the waves to cease their movement toward him. The waves and the tide continued to rise. In choosing Canute as our symbol, however, we are being a little unfair to him. According to legend, Canute was a devout man who wished to prove to his people that even a king is powerless before God and Nature. Unlike his courtiers, he understood ebb and flow. Yet there are people who, for reasons of personal psychology, take as literal truth our culture's romantic ideal of unchanging love and attempt to use it as a rigid guide to real intimacy rather than to hold it loosely as an inspiring but flexible story. They invoke the power of Love to halt a natural cycle, just as Canute's courtiers invoked their king, only to see the waves rising about their idols. Returning to Ainsworth's categories, their attachment style may be anxious like a Casanova, but it might also be avoidant—having found love against all odds, they feel deeply pessimistic about ever regaining it, should it even briefly slip from their grasp.

Curiously, one place to find such individuals these days is among couples who remain together over years or even decades but avoid marriage. Scattered in this diverse group among free spirits who wish to leave their options open and chronic doubters who cannot trust themselves to make a decision are a fair number of people who fear that any movement in their relationship, even movement toward marriage, will destroy it. Even more common are the couples who treat time and change as the sworn enemy of love. They would save love by embalming it or, to move from the archaic language of Victor Hugo to an old instant coffee commercial, to freeze-dry it "at the peak of perfection." The dream is the same as Casanova's, or perhaps of all lovers: a love suspended in time with no beginning or end. The freeze-driers make a paradoxical move as they reach for that impossible goal. They try to preserve freshness and novelty by stopping time and banishing change. Sometimes such a para-doxical move actually works. A divorced man of fifty-nine (Edmund Morris from Chapter 7) who has lived unmarried with a woman for the past fifteen years told us, "I love Carol more than ever and I think that's because we never married. When I was married, each of us took the other for granted and it became stale. Carol never ceases to fascinate me." More often, the relationship begins to develop the eerie rigidity of a face that has had too much plastic surgery to preserve its "youth."

One such relationship was the marriage of Gail and Henry Jackson (discussed briefly in Chapter 1). They were high school sweethearts in a small blue-collar town. He was a popular school athlete; she was an equally popular cheerleader. They began dating as sophomores, were go-ing steady by their junior year, broke up to date other people, but were the first of their "crowd" to be married, at the age of twenty. They were excited by each other, thrilled by their romance, and delighted to find themselves married. Though it may sound like a preadolescent's ro-mance novel, the story is true. It is also incomplete. Each was inwardly fearful of the world they faced together as they emerged from their com-fortably small community. Despite an easy popularity in high school, they each felt uncomfortable in social situations, uneasy with too much intimacy, and insecure about their abilities to "make it" in the world. Gail secretly feared that her youthful beauty was her only valuable at-tribute. Henry was afraid that he would never live up to the high stan-dards of his revered grandfather, a self-made man who had earned the respect of his extended family and the larger community.

Gail's response to this moment of precarious bliss was an attempt to freeze it into a timeless moment that would stretch on forever. She was determined to "lock-in" her relationship with Henry at the peak of their shared romantic triumph. She became a vigilant guardian of the inten-sity of their love. Her "distance alarm" was set to maximum sensitivity. Any waning of Henry's attentiveness was a sign of imminent catastro-phe. Any decrease in the frequency of love-making was a searingly hurt-ful abandonment. There was no such thing as a natural ebb and flow of attention and intimacy, only a series of potential disasters barely averted by a mix of seductiveness, charm, and complaints. Gail did not battle against all change. They had four children. She was a devoted mother.

She threw herself into the progressive improvement of home and garden. The flow of time was welcome as long as it did not carry Henry and her away from the days of the courtship.

Of course, like Canute, she failed. Henry felt increasingly angered rather than held by her romantic demandingness. His growth and progress became a problem for her as he overcame some of his anxieties, became more comfortable with others and with himself, and dared to create a small business that was a modest success. All this made Gail happy and proud, but she could not tolerate the periodic shifts of Henry's attention away from her that it required. She slipped into a mild depression and spent more of her time immersed in sexual fantasies that recaptured the bliss of earlier times. When Canute's strategy failed her, she was tempted by Casanova's. She ended up in individual psychotherapy, which was soon converted to couples' therapy. Some of Gail's desperation around sexual attention and intensity was connected to the particular details of her history. As a young girl, hidden in the closet of her best friend, she had repeatedly witnessed incest between her friend and the friend's father. The sight left her with bewildering feelings that included disgust, excitement, and a troubling regret that her own father was not interested in her in the same way. The regret had as its background the much more ordinary experience of feeling a bit marginal within a large family, in danger of losing the attention of those she loved, fearful that their attention, once lost, would be lost for good. Even as a child, she had no trust in the natural ebb and flow of relationships. Finally feeling cherished by Henry through their courtship and marriage, she was not about to trust it as an adult.

Where was Henry in this? His efforts to freeze time were not focused on the nature of his bond with Gail but on Gail herself. He was all for change and growth in his life, but Gail was to remain untouched by it— safely cloistered at home, dependent, insecure, and devoted. He kept family finances completely out of her view, controlling her spending through a weekly cash allowance that was her only source of funds. As the children grew older, he complained that Gail was not doing enough and should take a part-time job, but at the same time he criticized her and questioned her abilities, steadily undermining her already shaky self-confidence and further entrapping her at home. He scrutinized her behavior just as intently as she studied his but with a different concern. He searched for signs of infidelity in her actions or simply in her desires. He examined every encounter she had with another man as a possible flirtation or seduction. The only hope he had for peace of mind was to have Gail remain forever the insecure but rapturous teenager he had first loved. Any move she might make to enter the world more confidently only increased the danger, however much he might berate her for her fearfulness. Henry was every bit as frightened by the natural ebb and flow of closeness as Gail was, but his fear took the form of pathological jealousy.

Enter Othello

To Casanova and Canute, we must add another character who fights the tides, the figure of Shakespeare's Othello, a symbol of all-consuming jealousy that transforms any movement into a betrayal. In an earlier chapter, we spoke of the value of a modest and forgiving jealousy within a loving relationship to provide an alarm system that brings about reengagement before a drift apart goes on too long. If jealousy is to function as a helpful alarm rather than a destructive force, however, the jealous person must let himself be quieted and soothed, must allow a reengagement that is, in the end, loving rather than hateful. Othello's jealousy, relentlessly driven by the envious whisperings of Iago, was created to destroy rather than to safeguard love. Iago made that outcome certain by systematically attacking each reassurance offered to Othello by his wife Desdemona. Henry too could not permit himself to be comforted. Trust would destroy his vigilance and make him vulnerable to hurt and to loss. His jealousy became an impenetrable barrier to reconciliation rather than a reason for it.

To fully understand the elements that spawned Henry's internal Iago, torturing him with whisperings of his wife's infidelity, one would have to examine his development in detail. Certainly, he had struggled with self-doubt throughout his life, inspired and oppressed by the figure of his grandfather, a skilled artisan who was revered by both family and community. Henry was acutely aware of his own limitations. In his anxiety, he amplified them in his mind. Henry also knew his wife, however, even if he could not quite put his finger on what it was that he knew. He seemed to have an intuitive grasp of Gail's hidden fantasy life, even though she never spoke of it to him, and he feared that her unspoken desires would carry her away from him. Over many years of marriage, they had found no language that seemed safe enough to let them address this danger directly, no way to share the separate tensions that each bore alone, no way to begin a movement toward each other and repair the increasing estrangement. Each word that might be spoken seemed as though it would shatter their marriage and bring about a catastrophic loss for each of them. So, over time, fewer and fewer words were spoken. What remained were bursts of anger and accusations.

Loss and Faith

At the core of each of these stories is the issue of loss. At the core of the human condition is also the issue of loss, along with the pain of confronting it. What unites the character types who fight the tides, the Casanovas, Canutes, and Othellos, is their desperate attempt to make the shadow of loss disappear from their lovers' Eden, a determination to live in a world before the Fall made loss an abiding part of human experience. Each struggles to create a way of loving that is free from the possibility that love may be painfully lost. Don't all lovers long for that? What lover does not strive to make love last? These particular lovers, however, share an essential lack of faith that makes even ordinary uncertainty intolerable. These lovers are unable (or perhaps unwilling) to trust that a beloved who is momentarily drifting away will not inevitably disappear forever. If we return to the "strange situation" as both metaphor and prototype, when the beloved has left the room, there is no reason to believe that he or she will ever return. In the language of developmental psychology, we are describing individuals who lack object constancy, the ability to hold in one's mind a reliable picture of a person who is not there.[12]

It may help to think about the experience of riding a roller coaster. Individuals who enjoy it have faith that the ride will end safely, that the dips don't really mean the car is out of control and headed for a crash. For others, no matter how joyful the screams around them, when the bottom drops out, the car tips down, and their stomachs rise up into their throats, they are so overwhelmed with dread that they swear never to take that ride again. There are people for whom the natural ebb and flow of closeness in loving relationships feels like that kind of roller-coaster ride. Some people are so filled with dread that they spend a lifetime skirting all intimacy. (The diagnostic term *schizoid* is sometimes used to describe these individuals.) Others with a little less fear or simply a stronger longing for closeness and attachment will take the plunge, but only if they can put in place a stringent "risk-management" strategy to reduce the threat of loss. We have described three of the most common strategies in this chapter. On its own terms, the Casanova strategy is probably the most successful. In skillful hands, it can create an ongoing series of joyful and exuberant moments, though the complex satisfactions of sharing love and responsibilities over a lifetime must be sacrificed. The strategies of Canute and Othello fail even on their own terms. They simply don't work. In their fearful denial of the natural harmonic motion in lasting attachments, they make the bond of love so rigid and brittle that it almost always shatters. They end up creating what they most fear. Their strategies are self-fulfilling prophesies. In the end, their latest experience will confirm once again the wisdom of their deep mistrust of loving attachments. A better approach is to understand the naturalness of ebb and flow in all close relationships and to reckon with it respectfully but without unnecessary panic or premature catastrophizing. That strategy is a much more reliable way to reduce the risk of lost love.

As a child, one of us was told a story by a Russian neurophysiologist. Two mice were perched on the edge of a bucket of cream, stretching their heads down to get a sip. They both slipped and fell in. Neither one could swim. The sides of the bucket were too slick and too high to climb over without a solid surface to stand on. One mouse realistically assessed their predicament, concluded it was hopeless, gave up, and drowned. The other mouse was furious, began thrashing at the cream in his rage, turned it to butter, and climbed out of the bucket. The story, although originally told to illustrate the adaptive value of emotions, also conveys the importance of hope and persistence. A fascinating series of studies have examined cognitive processes in people with and without depression. A remarkable conclusion emerged from those studies. In certain important ways, depressive thinking is more realistic than "normal" thinking. It just happens not to be very adaptive.[13] We don't want to carry optimism too far. Only a fool of a mouse would willingly dive into a bucket of cream. There are genuinely hopeless situations and there are genuinely hopeless marriages. For a marriage to survive as something vital and satisfying, however, there must be some give in it and enough faith in the resilience of the bond to be comfortable with its motion. The individuals (and the character types) in this chapter have all developed strategies to protect themselves in the absence of that faith. They lack a fundamental optimism about human relationships. Such optimism may not always be warranted, but its absence almost always creates the very unhappiness that these tide-fighters suspect is just around the corner.

9

Friendships and Marriage
Risks and Rewards

"I am looking for friends [said the little prince]. What does that mean—'tame'?"

"It means to establish ties . . ." said the fox. "To me, you are still nothing more than a little boy who is just like a hundred thousand other little boys. And I have no need of you. And you, on your part, have no need of me. To you I am nothing more than a fox like a hundred thousand other foxes. But if you tame me, then we shall need each other. To me, you will be unique in all the world. To you, I shall be unique in all the world."

Antoine de Saint-Exupéry, *The Little Prince*

Examined closely, all personal connections show signs of an ebb and flow of closeness over time. Friendships follow the same pattern, although the rhythm of the movement and its long-term consequences often differ from drifts in romance. Although this book's focus is on committed romantic relationships, a more detailed look at friendship is crucial for several reasons. First, a better understanding of ebb and flow as a general pattern in all relationships deepens our understanding of its workings in romance. In particular, it sheds light on the effect of covenants (such as marriage vows) in the trajectory of relationships. Second, friendships serve an important stabilizing function in a marriage. They take some of the pressure off each spouse to be all things to the other. They can also satisfy the craving for novelty within the context of a secure marriage. Third, friendships have the potential to demolish the most cherished marriage when the experiences of tidal drift are misunderstood. It is not easy to balance our wish for new or multiple close relationships against the fear of ruining those we hold most precious.

Start with the idea that friends, like lovers, are always moving closer together or further apart. Such movement is harder to spot in friendship because it tends to be both glacially slow and free from the high drama of romance. The only significant exception to this universal law of motion in friendship is "acquaintanceship" within traditional societies, where movement is masked by formal affiliations that are role-based and rule-bound rather than "personal." The writer John Bayley portrays such a social world in Oxford during the 1950s:

> That was particularly true in Oxford, still an academic society, in which one could be on good terms with a large number of people, meeting them most days in college, at dinner in hall, or in lecture rooms and laboratories, without having any idea of how they were situated domestically, or socially, or sexually. Other people's lives might have seemed intriguing, which was part of the fun of privacy, but they remained what was on the whole an accepted and comfortable blank.[1]

Notice, however, that Bayley hints at internal movements of interest and curiosity. The emotional shifts are not absent; they are merely not permitted to affect visible behavior. In the United States, where almost all relationships are experienced as personal, these movements are regularly unmasked, become part of the visible interaction, and are often explicitly communicated.

It may help to return to the conversation between two former college roommates that we described in the Introduction. Carl and Richard were talking about drifts in marriage, but what about their relationship with each other? They met as freshmen roommates on the first day of college. Their friendship has lasted to their lunch together more than thirty years later and both men expect it to extend into the indefinite future. There have been no real breaks in their friendship, no periods of estrangement, no time when a call from one to the other was not welcomed. Over the first decade, it felt absolutely constant. Both Carl and Richard would have dismissed the idea of ebb and flow in friendships. Certainly, there were times when each man's attention was focused elsewhere, but any drift apart or together seemed so small as to be meaningless. Yet at a certain point, it became obvious that they saw each other less frequently, that the sense of detailed knowledge of each other's life was no longer there. Their time together became (for a while) subtly less satisfying, a change that they barely noticed but that nudged them further apart. Eventually, they were still loyal to each other but they were no longer as close. A decade of apparent constancy had hidden a glacially slow drift that finally crossed the threshold of awareness.

This pattern is very common in friendships—a tranquil period in which nothing seems to change and then the realization that somehow it has. Such recognition may come with sadness or a shrug. It may trigger corrective action or a sense that life has changed and one must get on with it. Either way, there is usually much less agonizing than when lovers drift apart, so the importance and complexity of the moment is often missed. Before we examine it in more detail, however, we must look briefly at the recent history of friendship. That will require separate discussions of men's and women's friendships, for they have developed very differently over the last century.

Differences Between
Men's and Women's Friendships

The standard sociological argument is that the rise of industrialism and the dominance of urban life toward the end of the nineteenth century caused the traditional rich network of communal connections with neighbors, friends, and kin to collapse, leaving marriage and the family as the sole haven within an atomized and competitive world. In the realm of friendship, a deeply embedded interdependent life was replaced by relatively shallow "socializing." Certainly, there is truth to this broad outline, but more recent scholarship suggests that the story may fit men better than women. This revisionist view is well represented by the book *Best Friends and Marriage* by sociologist Stacey Oliker.[2] She argues, both from historical material and her own contemporary studies of women's friendship, that friendship has remained vital and central to women's experience, despite the emergence (in the late nineteenth and early twentieth centuries) of an idealized picture of romantic companionate marriage that meets all the emotional needs of both husband and wife. She describes married women who are deeply embedded in networks of friendships that (as we will explain later) help sustain their marriages rather than devitalizing them.

The picture is somewhat different for men. Oliker has found that, whereas women continue to form ardent friendships throughout their lives, men do not. Men rely on old friends and, as they age, their number of close friendships declines. That may be particularly true for "modern" fathers who are more committed than past generations to being involved in raising their children. In our own study of marital satisfaction and differing child care arrangements among couples with young children, almost all the fathers described a slipping away from their friends. Deeply committed to their children, deeply committed to their jobs (or to the income their jobs provided), they simply could not squeeze enough time out of the week to sustain a vital connection with friends as well. The problem may not simply be logistics. Feminist psychoanalysts, beginning with Nancy Chodorow in the 1970s[3] have argued that, because (overwhelmingly) women raise children, girls develop their first heterosexual attachments (to their fathers) within a sustaining matrix of same-sex intimacy, a pattern that they continue during their adult lives. Boys, who are also raised mainly by women, find caretaking and first heterosexual love in the same individual. As adults, they are more likely to seek complete emotional fulfillment in their "one true love." The optimistic prediction is that, as fathers become more involved in parenting, men will develop a greater capacity to combine marriage and friendship in their lives. But logistics do matter. Historically, married women, particularly women with children, have sustained friendships during the daytime hours when the men were at work. As women's careers, ambitions, and work schedules become indistinguishable from men's, the natural rhythms of friendship may become harder and harder to sustain.

Unrealistic Ideas About Friendship

Perhaps even more than romantic love, notions of friendship are often based on a motionless ideal that does not require anything so mundane as ordinary maintenance and adequate time. In boyhood stories, friends mingle blood and are forever blood brothers. In long-distance telephone commercials, a simple call reaffirms that two women are "Friends for Life." A 1986 survey confirms that the ad agency was attuned to current notions about friendship.[4] Most people assumed that best friendships are self-maintaining and based almost entirely on affection. They were expected to last without maintenance and relatively safe from damage by decreased contact—in contrast to marriage. The contemporary message that marriage requires "work" has clearly taken hold, but best friendships are seen to be immune from this burden.

Oliker describes the concept of "romantic friendship" among women that "developed parallel to romantic marriage, as its cultural twin . . . [and] absorbed the tension between the ideals and realities of nineteenth-century marriage."[5] Paradoxically a new ideal of companionate marriage was being proclaimed at a time when male and female worlds were in fact becoming increasingly separated. Women's romantic friendships picked up the slack. By Oliker's account, romantic friendships among women declined in the early part of the twentieth century for several reasons. Male-female companionship increased with the advent of education for women and, by the 1920s, dating "was an intensive and time-consuming leisure pattern . . . which isolated couples far more than the nineteenth century courtship or peer activity had,"[6] sapping energy from female friendships. Additionally, the spread of psychoanalytic ideas on the ubiquitousness of sexual feelings led women (and men) to look more closely at the erotic feelings behind romantic friendships and it was often more than they could bear. Oliker comments, "the 'lesbian threat' would hereafter shadow the course and culture of female friendships."[7] Finally, in the 1920s and 1930s, a new trend toward marital counseling developed in the wake of the increasing divorce rate. Marriage counselors emphasized togetherness (i.e., companionate marriage), in which husband and wife were each other's best friend, as the cure. Gradually, romanticized same-sex friendships between women faded, to be replaced by intimate but nonromantic friendships that supplement the friendship between husband and wife. Yet some of the romantic ideals of timeless constancy still cling to our images of close friendship and blind us to the actual contours of friendship as it is shaped over time.

The Skills of Friendship

For a friendship to flourish, each person must have the skills of friendship. Many people come to us in sad bewilderment asking why their children cannot make friends. These well-meaning and worried parents have no idea what skills their children must develop to make friendships possible. Apparently, the idea that friendship is a skilled activity takes a moment to grasp. We are fooled by the ease of certain wonderful friendships that, on closer examination, turn out to be held together by their contexts. Some circumstances, such as living together in a dormitory or playing on the same sports team, often function as a kind of social glue that temporarily keeps individuals in contact and involved with each other. Sociologists[8] refer to these relationships as "friendships of convenience." They distinguish them from "friendships of commitment" which outlive the context that created them. These are the skilled friendships. These are the friends who actually make an effort to contact each other, exchange news, spend time together, even try to be helpful to each other long after the easy situational glue is gone. The ability and the willingness to bear one's fair share of responsibility for initiating contact, to take the trouble to see that time is set aside to be together, and simply to show up when one said one would may not ordinarily be thought of as skills, but they can be learned and refined over time.

Although the expectations about friendship differ somewhat from culture to culture, two Oxford psychologists[9] have found that the following six friendship "rules" seem to exist in all cultures: stand up for a friend in his or her absence; share news of success with him or her; show emotional support; trust and confide in each other; volunteer help in times of need; and strive to make the friend happy when in each other's company.

Underlying these skills and behaviors is something that cannot exactly be taught, but it can be encouraged and cultivated. It is the ability to put oneself in someone else's shoes, the capacity for empathy. Without it, friendships shatter not only because someone without empathy inevitably hurts people's feelings, but because a person must seem to "feel for us" to feel like a friend.

Curiously, some people lack the skills of friendship even though they appear to be surrounded by people much of the time. A college professor who followed his success across international borders from one university to the next was often incredibly lonely although he was a popular teacher and seemed to have many friends. A student who knew him well was initially perplexed but finally understood his plight. He cruised from one country to another certain that his charisma, his wit, and his intellect would gain him an enthusiastic following among his colleagues and students, which it did. Over the long haul, however, these friendships of convenience were left behind. He had no lasting friendships because he had never mastered the skills of keeping in touch with old friends over distance and over time by phone calls, letters, and visits. Although he was rarely actually alone, his malaise and lonesomeness were just barely visible beneath his engaging social presence.

The Typical Course of Friendship

As a friendship is getting off the ground, it often moves at an accelerated pace, riding the same wave of excitement and novelty that we know well from romance. Stacey Oliker quotes a series of women talking about the sense of life transformation at the start of a new close friendship.

> I began feeling good about myself for the first time in a long time, which of course was very positive for my marriage. Oh, it was just a panacea for all my ills.
>
> It was a catharsis. To release all that was pent up. . . . That hour [spent together] was so exceptional in my life. It certainly turned me around.[10]

These sentiments parallel the joy and relief in finding a new romantic interest. A new friendship is like the best of crushes—we are thrilled to discover that the one we find so interesting is actually interested in us.

Once a friendship is well established, however, moments of surprise and discovery no longer cascade in. The sense of wonder begins to fade. Friends no less than lovers get taken for granted once the initial infatuation is over. We have described the tidal drifts that create a peak in divorce rates after three to four years of marriage. The cycle in friendship ordinarily takes much longer. Shifts in intensity are less dramatic when people see each other less often and spend shorter periods of time together. But sooner or later the best of friends begin to feel that they know everything there is to know about each other. An old hunger for freshness returns. The old friendship may feel precious and comfortable, but an openness to new infatuation starts to grow beside it. If one is found, it can siphon off so much time and energy that the old one just fades away. What looked like a friendship of commitment reveals itself, when stressed, to be a friendship of convenience. The stress need not be a newly blossoming friendship. It might be a move to a new town by one person or a new job, anything that refocuses energy, time, and interest in new directions. These events uncover the absence of a sustaining commitment or, to use another vocabulary, the absence of a covenant that gives friends both the authority and responsibility to "reel each other in" when the inevitable drift apart begins. An old children's round admonishes us to

> Make new friends but keep the old,
> One is silver and the other's gold.

The sweet rhyme reflects a very real conflict.

The conflict between the novel and the familiar doesn't mean that friendships can't last, just that they must reckon with the same tidal drifts as love. The anthropologist David Schneider wrote that "friends are relatives who can be ditched if necessary."[11] Yet the "if necessary," when closely examined, often turns out to be simply a misunderstanding of the natural ebb and flow in all close relationships. The natural cycle of close friendship seems to be on the order of a decade, unless at least one person "adopts" the relationship with an active devotion.

When some friendships made in childhood last into adulthood, the friends may take each other on as "false kin" and begin to behave as relatives for life. To quote Schneider, "relatives are friends who are with you through thick and thin . . . whether they do their job properly or not."[12] These friends are committed to the necessary maintenance work in friendship that they would put into a relationship with a parent, child, cousin, or even spouse. Returning to Carl and Richard for a moment, who were still lunching together at the beginning of the chapter despite periodic ebbs in the intensity of their connection, both are committed to active intervention to keep the inevitable future ebbs from becoming permanent. In friendship as well as marriage, the constant erosion from tidal drifts must be reckoned with if the friendship is to survive beyond the immediate circumstances that once made it easy.

Friendships that Grow "Too Close"

The close parallels between friendship and romance lead us back to a subject we have already discussed—the way that friendship can cross over into the realm of sexual excitement and represent a threat to marriage. A close friendship filled with "good chemistry" can head in the direction of sexual consummation without anyone realizing it unless there is an understanding of natural drift. That understanding must be coupled with a willingness to take action—to be willing to suspend a relationship or let it cool down—when sexual temptation appears to be just around the bend. It is a willingness to listen to the "closeness alarm" that we described in Chapter 3. These cautions were once firmly built into a social structure that was highly segregated by gender. Most (heterosexual) people in good marriages once found friendship with people of the opposite sex too dangerous for comfort. In a 1979 survey from *Psychology Today*,[13] 73 percent of respondents found cross-sexual relationships complicated by sexual tensions, social discouragement, and the fact that opposite-sex friends had less in common. Since then, however, the majority of women have entered the workforce in jobs that increasingly involve working closely with men on joint projects. The logical consequence is that cross-sexual relationships are now more common and less socially discouraged than in the past.

As gender-based segregation is left behind, the idealistic hope is that healthy marriages are not endangered by these extramarital friendships. That hope ignores the natural course of close relationships: in the excitement of the unfolding phase, the pleasures of shared experiences tend to spread into new areas (the "ripple effect" from Chapter 3). Usually in a friendship with someone of the desired sex, curiosity about intimate thoughts and feelings leads naturally to sexual curiosity. Pretty soon, what was once friendly interest can be transformed into passionate desire, especially in a culture that no longer attaches significant stigma to sexual affairs.

Many couples in which both spouses work outside the home feel, understandably, that restricting their friendships to one gender is absurd. How, they would argue, can you keep from becoming friends with close coworkers? Why would you want to avoid friendships that do so much to enhance the workplace with a sense of familiarity and intimacy? After all, if occasionally sexual overtones rise to the surface, doesn't that add a little zing to work that is often routine and boring? We're not in the Dark Ages anymore, they might say, where a women has to be kept hidden in the home because her man can't trust her to be seen by other men.

Unfortunately, this comfortable attitude is sometimes too cavalier and self-serving. It leads to many "accidental" affairs that can blindside perfectly healthy marriages. Yet these affairs are not really accidental, nor are the people involved unusually thick-headed. They are merely swept away by the natural drift toward progressive closeness that accompanies any unfolding friendship. The old-fashioned biblical language of temptation conveys an aspect of this process that is hard to express in more modern terms. Friendly intimacy is almost always playing with fire. We need not give up the warmth of the fire, but we should be appropriately vigilant.

Friendship Can Strengthen Marriages

Despite these important cautions, however, friends can simultaneously strengthen a marriage and function as crucial buttresses to marital stability in a variety of ways. The intensity of too much mutual dependence is diluted when each person has a bit of a "diversified portfolio" of intimates, a function that in the past was partly filled by close contact with extended families. Consider the following descriptions of spousal relationships during friendless periods by women who participated in Stacey Oliker's survey.

> It was the first time in my life that I ever used tranquilizers. . . . When he had to travel, I'd say, "Don't leave me." I think now if I'd had someone to talk to, all that might not have happened.[14]
>
> I was afraid to let him do anything without me. I felt trapped and blamed him, even though it was my fault. I wasn't happy any of the time, not even when I was with him.[15]

Most women feel happier in their marriages when they have close women friends. One reason, Oliker suggests, is that *all* the women in her study talked to close friends about their marriages or romances. Frequently, these conversations included a kind of troubleshooting that Oliker calls "marriage work . . . [referring] to reflection and action to achieve or sustain the stability of a marriage or a sense of its adequacy."[16] Often the result was a constructive solution to a marital problem that had eluded the wife alone.

Wendy Michaels is someone who might not have been able to stay married without a group of friends to "keep me sane." She has been married for thirty years to a "kind and decent man, who really is my rock. I know he'll always be there for me and I know that he loves me. I can't imagine ever leaving him, ever hurting that much. He's such a good man." Then why is leaving even a question? Because her husband Kevin is exceptionally reserved and emotionally inexpressive, whether with words or touch. He seems uninterested in creating a vital sexual relationship with her, and equally uninterested in creating external adventure in their lives through travel or other explorations. Wendy feels curiously mismatched with this taciturn, predictable man. Though reliable and responsible as a mother and a legal secretary, she sees herself as a fundamentally passionate and adventurous soul trapped in a dull marital routine. Her children are grown, the years are passing, and she fears her growing sense of discontent. She did once slide into an affair with her employer, their already intense involvement spreading into the sexual realm (along the path that we have already described), but her love for Kevin and her guilt made extramarital sex an anguished and unstable solution. A more lasting answer came from her friends. At a Catholic retreat long ago, she met four other women, some married, some not, with disparate jobs and life experiences. They became fast friends and have been meeting together, sometimes for an evening, sometimes for longer retreats, over two decades. They welcomed and reciprocated Wendy's emotional intensity. Here, too, Wendy found a companion for trips to some of the exotic places that she longed to visit. Her friends offered her an "out" from the stark choice between deprivation by remaining with her husband and deprivation by leaving him. Her women friends have allowed her not to ask more of her husband than he is able to give. It is not a perfect solution by any means, but

Wendy is glad that she has found a way to stay with Kevin since she feels they really do love each other.

As this example suggests, one of the ways that friendship supports marriage is by offering a partial solution to the problem of our craving for novelty and variety in relationships. Because of differences in the patterns of men's and women's friendships, the solution works better for women than for men. Women continue to form ardent same-sex friendships throughout their lives. Men tend to rely on a decreasing number of old friends as they age. Thus women's pattern of friendship tends "automatically" to include the spice of newly unfolding relationships. Stacey Oliker even speculates that there is a nonsexual motivation in men's extramarital affairs. "Sexual affairs with women may be men's route to ardent and intimate friendship."[17] We would add that a new ardent friendship solves the problem of our natural desire for novelty.

Friends also provide a very different kind of support for marriage. Friends bear witness on a marriage. Without witnesses, most of us tend to let things go. An easy example is the way people let a house or apartment get messy if no one ever comes to visit. A more sobering one is that socially isolated parents are more likely to abuse their children.[18] Witnesses help us to put the brakes on before we descend to our lowest levels in a fight. When we entertain people in our home, we usually wish to present ourselves at our best and hope for good feedback about the way that we have chosen to live. Similarly, when friends see us with our spouse, we would like our relationship to be in moderately good repair and hope that our friends will both like our mate and admire our relationship. Furthermore, a good-enough friend can help by providing perspective on our marriage. We can risk revealing the flaws in the relationship and get a much better sense of whether they are really as bad as we thought or, at times, much worse than we dared to admit.

Husbands Can Feel Left Out

Yet we must return to the important differences in men's and women's friendship patterns. Currently, men depend more on their wives to satisfy their needs for friendship than the other way around. Women must be aware of this asymmetry and remember how left out a man can feel when his wife is caught up in the excitement of a new friendship. If he thinks he is never his wife's top priority because she is so much more solicitous of her children and her friends, he may turn to an affair, not only from loneliness and sexual desire, but out of spite. A few encouraging words from the wife about how "you should see your old friends too" will *not* do the trick. We mentioned our study[19] in which almost all the fathers of young children felt that the dual demands of career and family simply left no time to maintain their friendships. Many men experience resentment from wives and children if they take time off for a round of golf or a game of hockey with friends and perceive a double standard in the importance that their wives place on time with their own friends. This asymmetry is one of the few ways women's friendships can weaken a marriage.

A partial solution is shared friendships between couples or between families with children of similar ages, which can become a joint friendship project that binds a couple together rather than sending them off in separate directions. Obviously, some balance is necessary. Couples flourish when they have a network of friends that includes both other couples and individuals. Since men are less likely to keep in touch with their male friends, they may particularly benefit from couples' friendships. As women's work schedules come to look more and more like those of men, however, and the daytime hours for women's friendships diminish, women may begin to require some of the same friendship remedies as men.

In the meantime, many husbands who have exhausting work schedules still want their wives to arrange a social schedule during the weekend, even if their wives work too. For example, John Wilton, a lawyer in a high-power law firm, felt that his backbreaking schedule exempted him from responsibility for arranging weekend get-togethers with friends. He thought his wife Martha should do all the planning and cooking, since she worked much more reasonable hours as a librarian. In theory, Martha agreed. In practice, working at the library and tracking her two children's school and athletic activities left her completely depleted by the end of the week. She felt that her husband unfairly demeaned her job simply because she earned less money than he did. In fact, he frequently told her to quit because her job left her too little time for the family. Martha felt that John's real goal was to be able to control all her time, and she had no intention of placing herself "under his thumb" to that degree. Soon, planning the social schedule became a real bone of contention. It was the club that John wielded to pummel Martha into an appreciation of the insignificance of her job. He kept haranguing her about her topsy-turvy priorities that put the family second. They turned up at couples' therapy seeking a way out of their constant power struggle. "He thinks I'm his secretary," she would say repeatedly, and he finally got it. John came to understand that his way of asking Martha to handle their social schedule made her feel humiliated. Martha came to appreciate how much she missed seeing friends over the weekends and how her isolation had led to increasing bitterness. They built a regular evening out together into their weekly schedules. At a local restaurant, while they caught up with each other, they both planned weekend gatherings with friends. Martha and John each stopped feeling so martyred and alone.

One interesting facet of present-day culture is that many fathers with little time for friends become close to their teenage children in ways that seem more akin to friendship than fatherliness. Mothers, usually accustomed to being the parent who is closest to young children, can feel quite left out during this phase. The rift can be amplified if the father, pleased no longer to be the odd man out and feeling vague resonances to his own youth, joins his children in their adolescent rebellion against the mother. One mother commented to us, "I just didn't think I was going to be able to stand coming home year after year to my husband and teenage boys making their incessant off-color jokes and contemptuous remarks about women." Her husband denied that there was a problem until a friend of his wife's pointed it out to him.

Even when a father is close to his older children in a less destructive way, however, new bonds to children leave fathers prone to an "empty nest syndrome" that was once thought to be the exclusive experience of mothers. Fathers are often surprised by the powerful impact of a loss that has not yet become part of men's expectations. When feelings of sadness and depression sweep over them as children prepare to leave home, they may well feel bewildered by the sense of losing their best friends. At dinner recently, a friend of ours described the painfully empty year after his daughter left for college. "I just didn't see it coming," he added. "It was much harder on Bert than it was on me," his wife Beatrice agreed. For the years that their children were at home, she had limited herself to part-time employment to be more available and involved as a parent. During those years, Bert had intensely and successfully focused on his career. The unexpected result was that Beatrice, who had also used her more flexible schedule to maintain a robust network of friendships, was cushioned by them from the impact of the children's departure, while Bert awoke to a painful sense of isolation.

Friendship in an Extended Family

Amid these complex intergenerational cross-currents, couples who are lucky enough to have extended family nearby have a special privilege. Although the currents may be even more complicated, the turbulences often cancel each other out and bring about an overall smoothing of the flow. We first noticed this effect in a family brave enough to plan a three-generation trip for their summer vacation. Despite initial nervousness, they found that the concentrated intensity of a nuclear family traveling alone was happily defused by the presence of grandparents. When things got too hot, they could rearrange themselves into new and more comfortable groups. Families with extended family members living nearby have an automatic pool of what we might call friends with a covenant. Recall David Schneider's comment that "relatives are friends who are with you through thick and thin . . . whether they do their job properly or not." The prevalence of family feuds and other family horror stories prove that the covenants are not watertight, but each nuclear family relationship is not quite so precarious when an extended family is around with its varied possibilities for other varieties of intimacy.

Most people are willing to ask favors or impose on family members in ways that they do not allow themselves with friends, precisely because they are confident that relatives will not simply go off in a huff. An important example is back-up babysitting, which makes child care a less precarious proposition. Parents are then not as incessantly stressed by the logistics of a tightly configured work-and-family care arrangement. Some would argue that the lingering unpleasantness of old relational patterns like sibling rivalries or grandparents' favoritism outweigh the purely practical advantages of close involvement with extended families, but it is also extremely useful for children to grow up with more than one vivid example of marriage, love, and child rearing. The more children see this natural variation, the more free they are to choose their own way in a complex world if their parents' choices don't feel right for them.

Creation of False Kin

For individuals who live at a distance from their extended family, sometimes it is possible to create a multigenerational extended family substitute, a bit like the false kin of an earlier age. Carol and George Hendin were lucky enough to have this experience with their babysitter's family. Mandy O'Donnell began to work for the Hendins when her son James was sixteen months old, just one month older than the Hendins' only child Jack. Mandy brought James with her to the Hendin home while Carol Hendin, a social worker, was seeing patients in her home office. The boys got along beautifully, and Carol soon realized that Mandy was one in a million—smart, funny, creative, and full of common sense. It was bliss for Carol to have another mother around every day to compare notes, to be reassuring when Mandy was worried and to share her own worries when they arose. Some advantages of raising children in an extended family compound or a communal living arrangement became clear to Carol, since her own experience was so enhanced by the O'-Donnells' presence. That presence soon came to include Mandy's husband Will. Both families spent time together and each family provided evening babysitting for the other.

About a year later, when the Hendins were starting to think about having a second child, Mandy announced that she was pregnant. The Hendins took this as a sign, got right to work, and four weeks later, Carol was pregnant too. The second babies were both girls and, like their brothers, one month apart in age. The two families began to feel that they were fated to be lifelong friends, leading richly intertwined lives. Mandy was very skilled at managing four young children at once. Each child's experience was much like growing up with a twin who happened to live in a separate house nearby. It even seemed the most natural thing in the world for Mandy to offer her breast to both girls when they were hungry and Carol was in the office with a patient. Both families were a little high on how well the arrangement was working out, feeling not like an employer and a nanny but like two families who had been thrown together by luck and landed in the most wonderful friendship. Their closeness was a testament to good "chemistry" and the power of a shared enterprise to knit people together.

By the time the girls were three years old, Mandy wanted a job that would use more of her creativity. She found it in the neighborhood nursery school that James and Jack had attended. Soon both girls went off to school with Mandy as their first teacher. But just as the children's world was enlarging to include new school friends, Mandy was also growing as close to some of her fellow teachers as she had been to the Hendins. It was the beginning of a change in trajectory so gradual and subtle neither family saw it coming. The progressive movement of the Hendins and the O'Donnells toward one another had shifted to a slow drift apart.

The children still played together regularly over the next five or six years, but the adults grew more distant once their daily lives were no longer intertwined. The Hendins spoke of their wish to see more of the O'Donnells, but recognized that the employer-employee relationship is not a lasting covenant and may have made truly equal friendship even more difficult. They also wondered if the fact that Will and Mandy were five years younger and, apart from child rearing, in different phases of their lives mattered as well. The children ended up in different schools, without everyday contact to sustain their connection. As the parents' involvement with the other family diminished, the children also stopped calling each other as often. Finally, the extent of the drift apart struck the Hendins with forceful clarity as their children entered adolescence. They heard from a neighbor that Mandy was leaving Will after fourteen years together. The rumor was that she had left him for a woman but, by this time, Carol felt too awkward to call and ask, having heard nothing from Mandy directly. Being left at the end of the grapevine made Carol feel very distant from Mandy; no doubt, her not calling confirmed the distance in Mandy's mind.

The Hendin family's experience powerfully demonstrates the preciousness of "false kin" and how, in the crunch, they still differ from "true kin." It forces us to grapple with the fact that friendships, even between families, are not necessarily timeless. Instead, a friendship lives out a natural course and then, if one person wants out, there isn't much that anyone else can do about it. With no vows or blood ties to invoke as part of an abiding contract, shifting personal circumstances offer a hundred reasons for letting a friendship go. Catherine Schine's novel *The Evolution of Jane* tells the story of a childhood friendship that ended for inexplicable reasons. It is a wonderful meditation on the mysteriousness of this phenomenon and our desperate efforts to make sense of it. But that mystery does not negate friendship's preciousness. The bond between the Hendins and the O'Donnells made their shared decade more vivid and alive for all of them. That remains no less true even if the memories are now tinged with sadness.

The connection between these two families was what is sometimes called (with ominous tones when tracking abuse and exploitation) a "dual relationship." It bridged the realms of work and friendship, embedding purely personal goals in the employer-employee structure. Dual relationships are worth a little extra scrutiny because they are so common in a society that prides itself on being both informal and classless (at least in its ideals). We have already examined the dangerous ways in which dual relationships can become sexualized. When unequal power enters the picture, the potential for abuse is obvious. Yet, handled carefully, they may also be a source of novelty that sustains rather than threatens a marriage. Stated most provocatively, if each member of a couple has a job or an avocation that allows mentoring, teaching, or "showing off" to an appreciative audience, the wish to seduce and be seduced can sometimes have a socially appropriate outlet. The most innocent version of this solution is the joy of teaching our children about the things we love. In truth, most children nowadays don't accept much teaching or mentoring after age seventeen or eighteen (if we make it that far), so it doesn't hurt to have some other venue into which this urge can be channeled. The famously chaotic married lives of many celebrities may seem to cast doubt on this approach, but the seduction of a vast anonymous "public" is a very different phenomenon and would require a separate discussion.

Shared Projects Lead to Friendships

In *Overcoming Loneliness in Everyday Life*, we wrote extensively about the subject of shared projects and activities. We were particularly concerned with the seemingly obvious point that shared activities cause relationships to deepen without a whole lot of "trying." Since shared projects involve regular contact and interaction around a shared interest, they frequently trigger the natural tendency of relationships to move forward and therefore represent one of the better bets for developing relationships in a lonely life.

If a shared project involves either teaching or learning, it becomes even more exciting. As most good teachers know (but usually avoid mentioning), there is an element of seduction that must occur for teaching to "take." There is certainly a great risk of carrying this excitement too far, but there is also a great joy in being able to connect with others and help them to learn. By the 1970s, the problem of professors seducing students was so widespread and so discordant with emerging feminism that many universities created strict rules about sexual harassment to protect their students. But there are hidden complexities. Many of the teachers that students learn best from and remember as changing their lives are the most subtly seductive. They are the teachers who enjoy the unfolding of a new relationship that is required for a successful joint project of teaching and learning. Teachers who stay out of trouble can take pleasure in this shared movement toward another even as they understand that the relationship must come to an end long before the "unfolding" is complete. It is akin to specialized entrepreneurs who help a "start-up" company on its way, knowing that they will bow out long before the initial public offering. They enjoy the excitement of creating new relationships but, like most teachers, they recognize the inevitable loss at the end of each "academic year."

The adventure of connecting and then deepening a relationship is not unique to teaching. It is part of every shared project that involves regular contact and interaction. The sociologist George Homans noticed the same phenomenon in 1965, when he observed that "activities, interactions and sentiments are mutually dependent on one another and specifically, the higher the interaction between two or more people, the more positive will be their sentiments toward one another."[20] In other words, the more time people spend together engaged in a mutual activity, the more likely they are to come to like each other and to know each other deeply. This simple observation is an incredibly powerful finding that can be used to engineer new relationships into everyday life. Something as simple as a carpool or a regular walk together is likely to lead to an interesting new relationship. Although that new relationship may represent a risk to a lasting marriage, so does the absence of a range of relationships in the life of each spouse.

Friendship Matters

In conclusion, we can say that "extramarital friendships" powerfully affect the health of a marriage. They take some of the pressure off marriage to be everything for each person. To be each other's best friend, best sexual partner, and best teammate at the same time is a heavy burden and a bit of a long shot. Spreading out the role of best friend can help. A range of friends playing multiple roles in one's life can help even more. A mix of couples and individual friendships works particularly well. Couples' friendships can be a wonderful "joint project" to create novelty in a married couple's social life. Individual friendships offer an adventure on one's own that can eventually be shared with one's spouse, much as a story of one's travels might be. As long as proper respect is paid to the spouse's central position, the presence of friends allows some needs to be taken care of elsewhere. Despite the mix of idealism and indulgence in the concept of open marriage, however (or in its newer incarnation "polyamory"), the sexual relationship needs to remain exclusive if trust within the marriage is to be preserved. Over the years, we have seen too many people whose serious personal and political commitments to more open arrangements failed to protect them from the destructive effects of sexual jealousy. Therefore, friendships with strong sexual overtones need to be treated as dangerous to the marriage.

Joint projects with people outside the marriage, especially those that involve teaching or performing, may satisfy the need all of us have for adulation and the unfolding of new possibilities while remaining true to our marriage partner. These can be engineered into a life without much difficulty because we are a society filled with associations. There is an abundance of groups, organizations, and joint projects available for anyone who wants to take part. Lastly, people with extended families who live within socializing distance have the privilege of what might be called a "covenanted friendship" that often (but not always) has an extra chance of survival because of the protection in a blood relationship. In fact, when thinking about friendships and their trajectories, we should remember that they are likely to fade over time in our highly mobile society, lacking the formal promise that would allow friends to "reel each other in" when drift apart begins. Friendships outside marriage can be greatly enriching to married life, but contrary to our hopes, they should not be expected to last forever.

10

The Grass Is Always Greener (On the Other Shore)

Many people who hear our ideas about ebb and flow in marriage ask, "But what about couples who are always close?" Friends will tell us of times in their own marriages without any ebbs, just a wonderful closeness that lasted for months. When we ask for details about these times, they usually report playing and working together so closely day to day and depending on each other so regularly that there was very little opportunity to become estranged. Sometimes it was a long trip or a major shared project like building a house that quieted the rapid cycles of engagement and turning away. The very preciousness of these remembered times confirm that they were high-water marks left by the slower-moving tides of closeness. We are confident that these times contained little ebbs as well, some of them intuitively corrected in the moment and others lost in the warm glow of happy memory. But each of these couples had the tantalizing impression that if they could achieve steady closeness for a while, it must be possible for others over a lifetime.

Evidence for this odd conclusion did not come from real life. It was stitched together from images out of movies, television, novels, and magazines, along with the occasional glimpse of real people to create a lovely fantasy of the perpetually green grass on the other side of the fence. Alongside the ethereal ideal of romantic myths, most couples seem to have a much more down-to-earth notion of how happy couples look in real life. If we look closely at these ideas, however, we find they still hover just a little above firm ground.

The Myth of the Perfect Couple

What characterizes the real-life couples who appear so perfect that they touch our dreams and our envy? First, they seem engaged with each other at all times, even in public settings where the job is to socialize with others. Second, they don't appear to bicker or experience the little "disconnects" that most couples regularly experience. Third, they use their bodies in casually affectionate ways (perhaps just a touch on the arm, a reaching for the other's hand) to keep each other from feeling forgotten in a crowd. They often have little inside jokes that reflect a shared private life and let them briefly enter it despite the crowd. These impressions are gleaned from public appearances. Real-life couples we interview (even contentedly close couples) never report this degree of connectedness holding up indefinitely. The images from public glimpses of private lives, enhanced regularly by the media, dovetail with our own longings. They have an incredible power over us, particularly the power to make us feel that we're living our life the wrong way, lost in our moments of distance or disconnection. We often feel that we are outsiders to the world of romance and marriage, with our jerry-built relationships that ebb and flow. Meanwhile, the insiders dance and drink champagne and gaze deeply into their lover's eyes.

Few of us can decide if we are happy without looking at our neighbors and imagining the parts of their lives we can't see. We usually rate our own happiness based on our notion of what the norms are. Part of the reason we compare ourselves with others so often is to get a sense of those norms, particularly for something as hazy as love. We often worry that our closely-held blueprint for how things should be in our significant relationship might not be realistic. Even after our hidden investigations of others' lives, however, we may still feel like outsiders, condemned to do things in our own slightly flat-footed neurotic way while we envy the privileged few for whom love is always romantic and easy. Our investigations are incomplete. Though flooded with data, we rarely get to listen to other people's private thoughts about the state of their own relationships. We judge from public appearances and fictionalized lives. We learn about other people's thoughts indirectly, by talking to them, reading about them, or watching movies and television. None of these give us a reliably accurate read on the true experience of a most jealously protected relationship. Nevertheless, we make our best deductions and are often extremely surprised by the divorce of an envied couple.

In today's psychologically minded society, we often blame emotional troubles brought forward from childhood for our failure to achieve constant love and happiness. Television talk shows might reassure us that others are maladjusted too, but to preserve our dreams, we rationalize that we see just the weirdos and that most people must manage love better than we do. The high divorce rate continues to shock us because it calls into question this standard assumption. Given the high divorce rate, it is remarkable how easily people still fall into the familiar pattern of feeling like a romantic outsider and imagining that an inner circle has a much better time of it. "The grass might be greener" thinking is very seductive. Only under its spell can we persuade ourselves that there are couples who never experience an uneasy sense of distance.

The popular novel *The Notebook* is a good example of how enjoyable the idea of unchanging intense love can be.[1] The book is Nicholas Sparks's fictionalized account of the love between his wife's grandparents. It is essentially a straight love story about a romance that begins when the couple is young and stays forever fresh even after the wife develops Alzheimer's disease. Sparks finesses the question of changes in distance along the way by telling the story of their early love and then jumping ahead to the nursing home. In each section, the love between them is intense and unabated. We are left to assume that during the long intervening years, they also loved each other in perfect harmony. Translated into twenty-four languages, the novel clearly hits a chord of longing in all cultures. It is pleasurable because it speaks hopefully to our wish for perfect romantic love. In the end, it leaves us feeling all the poorer, as we gaze over the fence at a love that seems to have none of the bumps and pitfalls of our own messy real-life relationships.

Our attachment to the notion that there is a group of romantic insiders who are much more adept at running their lives tricks us into believing other couples' public images. In our psychiatric practices, we regularly listen to men and women who get depressed when they are with their spouses at parties or in restaurants. The couples around them seem more interested in conversation than they feel. Meanwhile, some of the same couples are probably looking back at them just as enviously. We are all too ready to accept outer appearances as the whole story for others, even as we know full well that our external appearance is less than half the story. By adulthood, we have all learned how to put on a good act. Many of us look quite content when we place ourselves in public view, whether we are or not.

Living in a culture that believes in the infinite perfectibility of self and relationships, people are misled into thinking perfection is achievable and that the loving couple at the next table probably has reached it. One of our worst fears is that this book could be misread as a guide to perfect love. Instead, our main point is that all relationships by their nature are subject to drift and distance. We hope that this secure knowledge will make people less likely to panic and run whenever they perceive distance in their own marriage. Once the universality of tidal drift is acknowledged, our norms can shift to encourage rather than undermine our efforts to turn the tides.

Threats to the Institution of Marriage

One would expect that the "grass is greener syndrome" would be less likely to flourish nowadays. For anyone whose ear is to the ground, there is much evidence that marriage as an institution is in trouble. In fact, we easily hold two deeply opposing views in our seemingly rational minds. The bitter conviction that no present-day marriage has a prayer of lasting "till death do us part" can sit comfortably beside a jealous certainty that other couples are living in the marriage of our dreams.

The National Marriage Project at Rutgers University has recently released a report titled *The State of Our Unions: The Social Health of Marriage in America*. It begins with a compilation of statistics from the Bureau of Census, the Center for Demography at the University of Wisconsin, the Survey Research Center at the University of Michigan, the George Gallup Research Institute, and other sources:

Key social indicators suggest a substantial weakening of the institution of marriage. Americans have become less likely to marry. When they do marry, their marriages are less happy. And married couples face a high likelihood of divorce. Over the past four decades, marriage has declined as the first living together experience for couples and as a status of parenthood. Unmarried cohabitation and unwed births have grown enormously, and so has the percentage of children who grow up in fragile families.[2]

Specifically, the report makes the following points. 1) Marriages are much more likely to be broken by divorce than by death. 2) Even though one might expect that a greater freedom to leave would mean that the remaining marriages would be happier, they are not. 3) Marriage is losing much of its importance as the central rite of passage from adolescence to adulthood; instead cohabitation is the more likely path. 4) Because people marry later, exit marriages earlier, and avoid marriage altogether more often, Americans spend much more of their adult life in a state of singlehood. 5) Women are much less confident that marriage is a likely path to happiness and success; instead, they are more accepting of cohabitation and child rearing out of wedlock.

The Embarrassment of a Happy Marriage

These sad statements about the state of marriage in our country mean that couples with excellent marriages may feel a bit embarrassed about it, as if they were missing some important contemporary experience by feeling happy with their partner. The spirit of our times pushes us to speak more frankly about what is psychologically wrong with our lives than to celebrate what is going right. Even the language of marriage and the happiness it can bring begins to sound passé. Many adults superstitiously avoid talking about their personal triumphs, be it children who are doing well or love relationships that are thriving. The popular books on marriage have titles like *Men Are from Mars, Women Are from Venus*. As *The State of Our Union* puts it:

Marriage has lost broad support within the community and even among some of the religiously faithful. In some denominations, clergy avoid preaching and teaching about marriage for fear of offending divorced parishioners. Marriage is also discredited or neglected in the popular culture. Consequently, young adults who desperately want to avoid marital failure find little advice, support and guidance on marriage from the peer culture.[3]

We are surprised by how quickly a spreading discomfort has left many people afraid to use the very word *marriage*. A twenty-eight-year-old child psychiatrist brought up in a strict religious family that vigorously condemned sex outside marriage told us that she now avoids the word marriage when talking with patients because she is sure it will anger some of them. Besides, she says, "the whole idea of marriage makes me feel queasy."

As Barbara Dafoe Whitehead (codirector of the National Marriage Project) points out, back in the 1940s and 1950s the etiquette books by Emily Post didn't even contain a separate chapter on divorce, but instead included divorce among miscellaneous topics at the end of a seven-hundred-page volume. Whitehead concludes that "within the larger framework of social relationships, therefore, the experience of divorce remained ill-defined, unelaborated, and unmediated. The very meagerness of the associated vocabulary had a dampening and isolating effect."[4] Now, in widening circles, it is marriage rather than divorce that must be spoken of quietly, if at all. To protect the feelings of the divorced and unmarried, we begin to avoid the familiar language of marriage. Meanwhile, without the old developmental milestones of engagement, marriage, and child rearing, young people are not sure what to aim toward. Adults with happy marriages do these young people a major disservice if we keep the details of our comfort within married life an embarrassed secret.

The word *marriage* is very hard to get rid of, despite periodic efforts to do so. We simply have no other language to describe a lasting intimate union between two individuals that seems to do justice to the experience. A fascinating consequence of that dilemma is a book by journalist E. J. Graff titled *What Is Marriage For?* She provides a rich and intriguing view of the history of marriage as an institution, but the book was written out of an urgent personal need. Graff (who is a woman) writes in her introduction: "And me? Early in my thirties, I married the woman I adore. . . . I became urgently determined to understand what we had done."[5] Here is how she summarizes what she learned:

> Marriage, in other words, turns out be a kind of Jerusalem, an archaeological site on which the present is constantly building over the past, letting history's many layers twist and tilt into today's walls and floors. . . . And yet marriage has outlasted its many critics (critics ranging from Plato and Jesus to Engels and Ann Lee)—and has outlasted, as well, the doomsayers of so many eras who post marriage's obituary notice every time society talks about changing its marriage rules.[6]

The idea of marriage, even as it changes, evokes something that society (like Graff herself) is unwilling to do without.

Expectations and Marital Happiness

In the midst of change, however, expectations have everything to do with marital happiness. Even as we grow ever more pessimistic about marriage in general, our dreams of the perfect union—the one that we deserve even though it keeps eluding us, the one we think we have glimpsed at the next table in the restaurant—become more and more demanding. Once again, Barbara Dafoe Whitehead puts it well:

> From the mid-60s on, the affectional requirements for marriage ratcheted upward, the demands for emotional satisfactions in family life escalated, the pursuit of love connections took on a manic intensity. Marital happiness, like the definition of a good provider, turned out to be a highly elastic notion.[7]

Inflated expectations guarantee disappointment and encourage divorce.

Realistic expectations are particularly elusive for children of unhappy marriages. Someone whose parents looked miserable with each other but stayed together might feel quite liberated to live in an age in which people are not expected to stay together "for the sake of the children." But in that freedom, an unrealistic blueprint for romantic happiness is often cobbled together from movies, observations, books, and hearsay. Individuals whose parents actually divorced cling to the same misleading blueprint, knowing that even the adults who brought them up could not get a marriage to work over a lifetime. Marriage counseling books used to emphasize the norm of marital permanence. Now they are more likely to talk about a limited and contingent marriage vow. J. Randall Nichols, in *Ending Marriage, Keeping Faith: A New Guide Through the Spiritual Journey of Divorce* proclaims, "The marriage vow is sign, seal and vehicle of self-investment; it is not a 'promise' that even could be kept on the same order of promising to do this or that; it is a commitment to work in relationship."[8] Certainly with divorce so commonplace, we have fewer young people with any memory of marriage sustained over a lifetime or the confidence that it can be. But consistency is not a powerful force in our love lives. There are as many young people as ever soaring on romantic dreams of perfect love.

So what can we who believe in the possibility of lasting happy marriages do to publicize our confidence in it? This book is in part our response—an attempt to develop expectations that are based more realistically on the natural course of love over time. There are also strong arguments to be made that marriage is good for people. Whitehead presents what she believes is overwhelming evidence that children raised by two parents do better on almost all measures of well-being.[9] Glenn Stanton, in another proselytizing but thoughtful and well-documented book, *Why Marriage Matters*, presents equally convincing evidence that the married state enhances physical and emotional health.[10] Stanton draws on one segment of a much larger field of study. A vast body of research has demonstrated that people who are more socially connected live healthier and longer lives. One of the most reliable ways to create social support is to get married.

We reviewed the research on social support and health in a chapter of an earlier book about loneliness, and the connection is compelling.[11] We will only add one counterintuitive fact about married life and well-being here. The largest recent study of sexuality in America came to the following conclusion:

The public image of sex in America bears virtually no relationship to the truth . . . in real life, the unheralded seldom discussed world of married sex is actually the one that satisfies people the most.[12]

Although popular representations of marriage often portray the dulling of mutual affection over time, the relative security that marriage provides may be a significant source of emotional satisfaction as well as a comfortable context in which to pursue physical pleasure.[13]

This study was widely covered in the press when it first appeared, but it is easy to forget under the onslaught of popular images of sex.

Although we tend to take the ordinary fabric of our lives for granted (consider one cynic's dismissive response to the above study—"marriage lets us guarantee ourselves sex and turn our attention to more important things"), we should take serious note of the following caution offered in our local newspaper by a divorce lawyer:

All of you who are thinking about getting a divorce: Look around you. Stop thinking about what you do not have and what you do not get. Instead take note of what you do have. Note now, because once the divorce process begins, most of what you see will be gone. You take so much more for granted than you know. Children, family, friends, daily routes and routines, tangible surroundings—so many years have gone into building the fabric of your life.[14]

Married life continues to have a thousand hidden advantages, even if we have lost the art and vocabulary of talking about them.

Our Peculiar American Perspective

Americans are starting to sound as cynical about marriage as Europeans have for years. The similar vocabularies hide fundamentally different perspectives, however. The Old World cynicism about marriage has its roots in an institution that was often more devoted to the financial and political advancement of families than the freely expressed love of two individuals. Paradoxically, the high divorce rate in the United States does not represent a jaded view of marriage as much as a persistent ideal-

important causes of that sense of futility are an idealized fantasy of the romantic alternative, a cycle of hurt feelings, and the rustiness phenomenon. The most difficult challenge to a marriage, because it invariably brings all three into play at once, is an actual consummated affair.

A curious thing has happened to affairs over the last several decades. There has been a transformation of their meaning within a marriage. Nowadays, an affair is one of the most common reasons for divorce. In the United States, there is a widespread sense that when an affair does not lead to divorce, the "wronged" partner has made a weak and indefensible decision that elicits perpetual public humiliation. Yet not so long ago, an affair was an event that marriages regularly survived. The change has carried with it both good and bad consequences and is still in a state of flux. In England, Prince Philip was said to have conveyed to Prince Charles the same advice he had received as a young man: if a marriage favored by the family was not satisfying after five years, the man was free to seek love elsewhere. This advice, followed a generation too late, led to a very different result than intended. The story also highlights the steady evolution of marriage from a multipurpose social institution to a purely personal commitment. One wonders what effect Bill and Hillary Clinton's "nondivorce" after multiple affairs will have over time on this country's views.

In the midst of these changes, we believe it is important to retain some freedom of choice for the individual faced with a spouse's affair. Obligate divorce is no kinder than enforced marriage and no more certain to be the right choice. Think back to Jennifer and Harold Sorenz, the first couple that we discussed. Jennifer had become attracted to someone else (significantly, through shared professional activity). She assumed the attraction meant that her love for her husband was dead. She felt strongly enough about Harold to want to avoid "cheating" on him, with all its hurt and humiliation, so she moved quickly (we might even say prematurely) toward divorce. Later, when the divorce was final and her infatuation for the new man in her life had cooled, she was paralyzed with regret. She could not believe that she had wrecked her life with Harold out of what now felt like sheer fickleness. She could find no redeeming features in her choice to go off with a colleague. Harold was much more tolerant of her fickleness. He had told her on numerous occasions that he was not particularly jealous or possessive. He would have

ism, a determinedly optimistic view that perfection can be achieved if we just move on, leaving behind what doesn't work and give it one more try. Go west, young man, and make your fortune. Get a divorce and make your next union a perfect one. In our study of loneliness, we wrote:

> We need to remind ourselves that the first members of each family to emi-grate to America *had* to be "tie breakers." In choosing to embrace the ad-venture of starting fresh in a brand new place, they had to be willing to give up the comfort of being known, recognized, and tied into a larger family unit and its surrounding community.[15]

Our emphasis was on social behavior. Whitehead has recently ex-pressed a parallel idea concerning political philosophy: America was "founded as the result of a political divorce, and revolutionary thinkers explicitly adduced a parallel between the dissolution of marital bonds and the dissolution of political bonds."[16] Thomas Paine, the great pam-phleteer of American independence, wrote a treatise, "Reflections on Unhappy Marriages," having himself left behind in England not only its political system but a marriage. Our champion of political freedom elo-quently championed the freedom to voluntarily make and dissolve mar-ital bonds. He believed that people who chose their partners freely would be much less likely to exercise the "freedom to disband." White-head contends that since our nation's beginning, we have faced the problem of how to expand individual freedoms without encouraging in-dividual license. "The challenge for a democratic people was to uphold the freedom to divorce without inspiring promiscuous divorce," she writes.[17] The deep irony of American marriage is that promiscuous di-vorce is an expression of our hopefulness about marriage, not our pes-simism. The cumulative burden of so many idealistic individual quests for greener marital pastures, however, is that we stand on the brink of a collapse of reasonable hope.

11

When Divorce Seems Imminent

Four strong winds that blow lonely
Seven seas that run high
All those things that don't change come what may.
But our good times are all gone,
And I'm bound for moving on,
I'll look for you if I'm ever back this way.

Ian Tyson, "Four Strong Winds"

We have described the natural patterns of motion within lasting relationships, but not all relationships are lasting and not all of
them *should* last. Some marriages are destructive. Some marriages are relentlessly bleak and empty. Some marriages seem fated to fall apart despite the best intentions of each spouse. We have examined the riptides
that can disrupt the regular pattern of movement apart and reconnection that characterizes relationships that survive over time and we have
suggested strategies to reduce the odds of permanent estrangement. But
what of the moment when a sense of certainty about separation and divorce crystallizes out of the more ordinary jumble of fear and discontent? Is there anything that an understanding of tidal drifts can add to
this usually anguished moment?

Some readers might hope that we can determine when a divorce is
necessary, perhaps provide a clear formula (ideally based on a self-
administered quiz) to determine when drift and estrangement are be-

yond repair. Instead, we must confess that people often surprise us. Some couples whom we believed were well on their way to divorce with no turning back possible have gone on to share long and happy lives. Some couples whom we thought were basically well suited and destined to endure have divorced for reasons we that we never fully grasped. We are not unhappy about these failures of our crystal ball. Prediction in human affairs is, even at its best, a statistical business that can always be confounded by a particular individual's action or choice.

The Power of Stories

One research group reports that it has achieved great accuracy in predicting divorce (although the results of their single "preliminary" study have not yet been duplicated). Psychologist John Gottman and his team interviewed approximately fifty couples. They discovered that a careful review of how subjects described their marriage histories during the initial interview allowed researchers to predict with 94 percent accuracy which would be divorced three years later. Gottman writes:

> Through my research on couples I have found that nothing foretells a marriage's future as accurately as how a couple retells their past. The crucial factor is not necessarily the *reality* of a marriage's early days but how husband and wife currently view their joint history. . . . Quite simply, when a marriage is unraveling, we found that husband and wife come to recast their earlier times together in a negative light.[1]

But the effects clearly go in both directions. The stories we tell about our past also recast our understanding of the present and shape future actions. When a husband and wife remember earlier times in a negative light, the "memories" become an active presence in the marriage. Most often they are like a wedge, driving wife and husband even further apart. The stories and metaphors that we use to make sense of our lives are not inert embellishments, they are powerful agents. During a drift apart, the future of a marriage can hinge on whether the current estrangement is viewed as part of the natural cycle that sustains love or as proof that there was never any real love to begin with.

The most important advice we can offer couples who are tempted to make a rift permanent is to pause one last time and consider whether a cyclic story of ebb and flow might be more accurate. A second caution is to recognize that memories of past marital unhappiness can be used as instruments of torture in a self-perpetuating downward cycle of hurt feelings. In Chapter 2, we described the danger of ever-increasing hurt feelings leading to deepening estrangement. Resentful and blaming descriptions of the past are usually central to the enterprise. It can escalate into a game of "chicken" to see which spouse can drive the other closest to the brink of walking out. Although the contest may begin with an underlying wish to be proved wrong by a genuinely convincing demonstration of a spouse's love, the satisfaction of seeing the other squirm may become too great a pleasure to give up. When this shift from loving to sadistic pleasure in a marriage has occurred, the future is in fact bleak whether or not a divorce occurs.

Resentment and romantic idealization are intimately linked. Gottman describes what he calls "The Four Horsemen of the Apocalypse"—warning signs of serious marital trouble. These are criticism, contempt, defensiveness, and stonewalling. He feels these behaviors create cycles of nastiness, derision, counterattack, and silent rage that are the precursors of divorce. We would add that these behaviors are most often the dark shadows cast by a luminous idealization of what life would be like with someone else, real or imaginary. It carries with it a corresponding devaluation of the unlucky and imperfect spouse. Without an imagined alternative, individuals rarely end marriages except for those that are obvious catastrophes. Most often the imagined alternative is a new love (conveniently free from ebb and flow), but it can also be the satisfactions of a job, or even the "superior" understanding and empathy of a therapist.

Therapist as Ideal Spouse

Gottman points out that spouses frequently express contempt for their partner by rolling their eyes for an interviewer while the partner is speaking. The same behavior is common in couples' therapy. The thought expressed usually seems to go something like the following:

"We [the eyeroller and the therapist] both know that neither of us thinks like this benighted person and our superior understanding creates a bond between us that leaves him/her out." One of the dangers of all therapy is that patients may feel that they have finally encountered someone who gives proper importance to their views and feelings. The alert and helpful listening of a therapist should not be confused with a "real-life" two-way relationship. The formal arrangements of therapy are specifically designed to eliminate as much as possible the natural waxing and waning of a therapist's interest and attention. The built-in time limit of a session, the regular interruptions to pursue other concerns, and the fee serve to damp out tidal motions. Yet many people mistakenly use an experience in therapy to confirm that their devalued view of the marriage is correct. So we add another caution for the moment just before deciding to divorce: don't transform an experience of therapeutic understanding into a vision of lasting marital bliss.

Real and Imagined Alternatives

To more fully address the subject of real and imagined new loves at the moment before a divorce, we must extend our earlier discussion about the lure of fascinating strangers one step further. The temptation of a freshly unfolding relationship with someone new hangs over all marriages during times of waning involvement. If the drift apart goes on too long, either spouse may well succumb to the temptation, if not in the flesh, at least in fantasy. The stage is then set for a remarkable transformation. The drift and the difficulties within the marriage cease to be the crucial determinants of the marriage's survival. The growing fascination takes on a life of its own and develops its own momentum. The exciting novelty of new love eclipses the old. Under its spell, marital history is rewritten. The course of the new relationship (even if it is largely imaginary) becomes the primary determinant of the marriage's fate. Unfortunately, as we struggle to protect ourselves from troubling guilt about our unfaithful thoughts, we start to emphasize the defects of our spouse and the failings of our marriage, which then drives the process further. This series of mental shifts happens so quickly that we are often unaware of it, but it sets us firmly on a course toward separation.

Workaholism

A similar transformation can occur around work. Just as marital drift can lead a person to fantasize about someone else, it can also lead a person into overdrive in a job or career to escape the emotionally upsetting developments at home. The result is a complete disruption of the ordinary oscillation of interest between love and work, already precarious in many lives. Certain careers practically guarantee that disruption. There are many professions in which time off for personal reasons seems simply not to be an option. It is no accident that among the professions with the highest divorce rates are the following: physician, lawyer, air-traffic controller, nurse. Any job that requires relentless effort year after year with little time off can deplete the energy and reserves needed to cope with personal crises. The danger has been especially great when the job was to resolve an endless series of crises in other people's lives.

The problem is now expanding to a wider range of occupations. Sociologist Arlie Hochschild, in a recent study of workers at an unnamed *Fortune* 500 company[2], found that many parents work long hours no matter what their job seems to require because they feel overwhelmed by the demands at home. A vicious circle is then set up: as overstressed parents spend less time at home, their children get even more needy and home becomes even more stressful. Husbands and wives are often in competition with each other to see who can put in the most overtime. As Hochschild explains: "People generally have the urge to spend more time on what they value most and on what they are valued most for. This tendency may help explain the historic decline in time devoted to private social relations."[3]

Thus, people are working harder to escape the complex emotional and practical demands of home, but their absence from home only makes the demands worse. Along the way, husbands and wives become less involved in a shared world. The chances of shared interests or joint activities naturally reversing a drift apart decrease dramatically, simply from lack of easy opportunity.

The consequences are even worse, however. The effects of long hours at work are further amplified by what we have labeled the "rustiness phenomenon." Hochschild argues that many Americans are now less relaxed and secure at home than at work, a startling social transformation. One reason that workaholism is sounding the death knell of many marriages is that workers frequently feel like awkward strangers in their own home and in the company of their own spouses. Because none of us likes to spend much time in settings or activities that make us feel clumsy, the effect feeds on itself. Over the past two decades, the average American has added an extra 164 hours of work to each month's schedule.[4] The extra time may be officially resented, but it still makes the work setting a little more comfortable and familiar, while life at home becomes just a bit more trying and unnatural. When we add in the prevalence of divorce and the social complexity of "blended" families with children from previous relationships, it is not surprising to discover that home is exactly the place where many people feel most inept.

In the moment before a divorce, therefore, the lure and the effects of involvement in work deserve as close an examination as other possible romances. A final effort to avoid divorce would require channeling time and energy away from the familiar rewards and satisfactions of the workplace to a home life that has come to feel unnatural and to conversations that no longer flow smoothly. Once rustiness has set in, initial efforts to reengage will make each spouse feel clumsy. That clumsiness is the direct result of how time and energy have been spent in the past. Shared patterns of smoothly coordinated movement fade quickly when they are not regularly exercised. The old adage that "you never forget how to ride a bicycle" does not mean that the first hundred yards after many years will not feel hazardous and shaky. Similarly, the first shared moments after a prolonged separation are usually shy and awkward. The happiness of the most loving marital reunions are punctuated for weeks or even months by an intrusive awareness of the strangeness of the other, as military couples accustomed to distant tours of duty know well. The sense of strangeness is even more disconcerting when its cause cannot be safely located in geographical distance, which is partly why the insidious drift into work or a new love is so devastating to a marriage.

Affairs

Even with both partners fighting for its success, a marriage may still reach the point where its resurrection seems impossible. The three most

been willing to "wait it out"" until she came back. (This tolerance had its downside, which we already discussed.) But Jennifer had been so compelled by her own notions of pride and morality that she enforced them on Harold. She was unwilling even to consider giving herself time to test whether she really would be happier in another life or to let Harold choose to wait. She was certain that the hurt she had inflicted could not and should not ever be overcome.

Crisis Mode

Often the critical question to ask in the face of increasing thoughts of divorce is, "How much is the issue of hurt pride eclipsing other important matters?" If a sense of wounded pride has begun to dominate all other feelings, a sizable chunk of time and a serious effort should be devoted to allowing the wound a fair chance to heal, without the rift being spitefully prolonged by hurt feelings that are indulgently nursed and nurtured. A clear understanding of natural tidal motion in relationships can be a great boon to that effort. If drift is understood as ordinary and expected even in the best of marriages, the intensity of both guilt and blame when it actually occurs is dramatically reduced. We can also learn something by listening to the standard admonishments that parents and teachers give to children. Children are regularly told to get over their hurt feelings with a friend or sibling and just play calmly again. If children are part of the family picture, it would be nice if we could demonstrate to them that we practice what we preach, whatever the final outcome. Certainly, the consequences of a divorce are magnified by the presence of children. Jennifer and Harold did not have children. If they had, it would have been even more presumptuous for Jennifer to decide for Harold that his pride would be hurt too much for the marriage to continue.

Often, however, a marriage can feel like it is in terrible shape, possibly beyond repair, even in the absence of an egregious disturbance like an affair. The combination of little hurts and rustiness can transmute the usual comforts of a familiar relationship into something profoundly troubling, like a horror movie in which everything seems the same but . . . Nothing terrible has happened. You only know that many of the things you used to be able to count on as signs of a good marriage are no longer there. For example, being so much at ease with your partner that you almost felt like you were alone in each other's presence, but in a good way. Or knowing that you could bring up your worries in the middle of the night to the person lying beside you who, even though asleep, would try to wake up and reassure you. Or feeling that when the car broke down far away from home, there was always someone to call to rescue you. Or feeling wonderfully calmed by the other person's presence in bed. Or having someone know all your sexual likes and dislikes. If all the little precious signs of comfort are gone and you have no clue how to get them back, divorce may feel just as inevitable as it does in the storm after an affair. It may be time for a couple to move into a crisis mode either on their own or through couples' therapy.

The best response a couple can make on their own to a looming crisis is for each partner to focus on tasks and behaviors that lead to active reconnection and to maintain that effort for quite a while, without either person taking refuge in thoughts that take the form, "All this would be so much better if only I were with someone else." A shared project that demands serious attention and can't succeed without both people working together can help dramatically. Being lost together on a desert island might be ideal, but it so rarely happens and perhaps makes the stakes a little too high. We may have to settle for vacations to exotic places where each spouse is fully and jointly engaged by the novelty of the experience.

Whatever form it takes, each person must somehow get away from the usual long list of have-to-dos, the constant stream of petty distractions that a friend of ours once described as having your life eaten by ants. The get-away must provide both shared activity and the time to talk everything over, perhaps apologize for past hurts, converse about inner thoughts, and relax sexually. Each person may feel that the strangeness and self-consciousness will never lift, that comfort will never return. But often when a couple spends an expanse of time together sharing a variety of activities, they discover that self-conscious clumsiness and anxiety simply can't sustain themselves indefinitely. Physical and sexual closeness, if they are not rushed, can work magic on the movement of the tides, and each person will feel the sense of well-being that comes with being touched. Sexual satisfaction also has the well-known capacity to make another person's annoying quirks less bothersome. A quieter dialogue that moves beyond past hurt feelings can often begin.

Most people find it impossible to imagine freeing themselves from everyday chores and responsibilities to create this time together. That failure of imagination has a lot to do with why people sometimes watch helplessly while their most important relationship trickles away. At its best, marriage can function as the primary support for almost everything else in adult life. When it is in trouble, it must be recognized as an emergency requiring immediate attention. If a boat were taking water on the open sea, no one would go about the ordinary routines made possible only by the presence of an intact boat. In the moments before a decision to divorce, a couple needs to give each other their full attention. There should be the same single-minded focus that they hopefully would have if a child of theirs were in very bad trouble. Other concerns must be shifted lower on the priority list, no matter how much the world expects us to go about our ordinary lives without a hitch.

Couples' Therapy

If the estrangement remains perplexing and a couple still feels stuck, it may be time for couples' therapy. There are several advantages to this strategy. A couple no longer has to figure everything out all by themselves. A fresh and hopefully informed perspective is added. In an earlier chapter, we also discussed how a witness tends to add just a touch more decency to our behavior. But it may help, when choosing a therapist, to make inquiry into his or her philosophy on the topic of marriage. Does a therapist feel she is in the business of trying to preserve marriages or is she completely neutral (or perhaps even a bit hostile) toward the institution? A therapist who is disillusioned about the prospects of marriage in general working out may not be fully invested in helping you to preserve your own.

Couples' therapy can be very effective in breaking the barriers to actually speaking about the real issues in a marriage, but it carries its own dangers. For example, it may lull you into thinking that you have done your part simply by "working on the relationship" during the therapy sessions. Like piano lessons, couples' therapy requires follow-up and practicing between sessions for real learning to take place. There is also the temptation to passively give over the direction of sessions to the therapist. Even though training and experience allows certains patterns to be seen more clearly, a therapist can never know as much about you and your spouse as you do about yourselves. She may easily flail about in the dark, fishing for reasons to explain your estrangement when you know very well what started the cycle of hurt feelings. Often the hardest hurts to put on the table are the ones that we ourselves feel are small and petty. How easy it is to divert attention to some other outrage that looks more respectable but leads the therapy away from the heart of the matter. If you are too proud to bring up what *really* hurt your feelings, your spouse will never have the crucial knowledge that would make it possible to correct his or her actions. Meanwhile, the couples' therapist will bumble along trying to figure things out to no avail, since you have withheld what matters the most.

We emphasize the downward spiral of hurt feelings because it is so common and so sticky. Like flypaper, once you touch it, every movement just seems to get you more tied up. Even a "neutral" external event like a job loss or sickness can easily lead to someone's feelings being hurt. We all have our notions of how a spouse should treat us when we are in distress. These expectations are so deeply embedded and often just childish enough that they are almost never put into words. In our work with couples, we frequently encounter people who look like they would rather die than admit the small things that have hurt their feelings. To conceal what they consider "babyish" about themselves, they act aloof and angry. They may even go on the counterattack, a time-honored diversionary maneuver. Meanwhile, their spouses don't know what hit them, since the hurt that began the whole cycle usually flew by unnoticed.

For the moment, men are still more likely to hide what really hurt them. As our colleague William Pollack vividly describes in his book *Real Boys*,[5] our society's pressure on boys to be tough leaves them relatively oblivious to their own feeling states. Even if hurt feelings are recognized, the worst failing is to act like a crybaby. Many husbands in couples' therapy honestly can't remember why they are hurt and mad.

The poor wife and the couples' therapist may sit around trying to figure out what started the cycle, but whenever they get "warm," the husband issues a blanket denial that he may very well believe himself. For a while at least, everyone is thrown off the trail. The result is a progressive deterioration in the marriage that seems to have no clear beginning and no good reason for it. A skillful couples' therapist can often help unearth the buried slights, but the process moves along much faster when both spouses come clean. When divorce is looming, time matters very much.

Couples' therapy can provide a jump-start to a couple's attempt to figure out what has gone awry in their marriage. It can also serve as an important signal to them that they are in the midst of a serious crisis demanding careful attention and time. When couples' therapy itself seems stalled, it is demoralizing but not definitive proof that a marriage is beyond repair. It may be that the match between a couple and a particular couples' therapist is wrong. The solution may be for the couple to divorce the therapist rather than each other. We have seen couples who left therapy "prematurely" but who nevertheless seem to have found the small but critical push that they needed to start solving problems on their own. Despite the value of a witness, there are certainly times when couples have a very reasonable wish to be rid of a third person looking over their shoulder. A couples' therapist should be a temporary help to a marriage, not a perpetual part of it.

Despite the best efforts and the best help, however, some couples will divorce. These days, many will. So many, in fact, that it is easy to surround oneself with people who are bitter and disillusioned about marriage. There are more than enough to go around, but it is dangerous to surround a marriage completely with such people. That is our final caution to those wishing to avert divorce. Marriage requires a social setting that supports it, not an inherently hostile environment. Some people claim that settings meaningfully supportive to marriage no longer exist. "We do not know a single person who is happily married," they tell us. Our response is, "Perhaps you are looking in the wrong places." But we concede that it may take a serious effort to locate the right place. Sometimes one must even lend a hand in building it.

Although the help of a couples' therapist is now readily available to troubled marriages, more fundamental and abiding aid is increasingly hard to find. The complex social web that once supported marriage and discouraged its dissolution is evaporating. It is not just that divorce is no longer taboo. That change at least could be celebrated as an increase in individual liberty. Marriage is rapidly becoming a socially stranded institution. It is no longer firmly embedded in a network of relationships that nurture it and help bear some of its inevitable strains. The hope that each spouse can single-handedly satisfy every emotional need of the other is more than most couples can bear. Successful marriages have always lived within a larger supportive network of family, friends, neighborhood, and religious congregation. They still do. The difference is that now the network must be actively sought out or, at times, even actively constructed by each couple. The social structures that support marriage are no longer routinely supplied by the underlying organization of our society. Maybe it is time to include a disclaimer with every marriage license: all necessary batteries are not included. Lasting marriages do not run on love alone.

12

Concluding Fears and Hopes

No man can struggle with advantage against the spirit of his age and country. . . . [I]t is hard for him to make his contemporaries share feelings and ideas which run counter to the general run of their hopes and desires.

Alexis de Tocqueville, *Democracy in America*

We begin our conclusion with three fears. The first is personal. The jokes have already begun. "So when will you get divorced? Everyone else we know who wrote about marriage has." Though these are our friends talking, there is always a deep satisfaction when "experts" stumble in their own backyard. And we hardly claim to be experts in an experience that we are still smack in the middle of ourselves. We have made observations that we believe are important and have organized them into a framework that we think makes sense, but it does not allow us to predict the future of a specific marriage, least of all our own.

Our second fear is that we are whistling in the dark, vainly struggling "against the spirit of [our] age and country," which Barbara Dafoe Whitehead has convincingly labeled a "divorce culture." It is not just divorce that threatens lasting connections. With increased economic and social freedom, particularly for women, more and more people have begun to protect themselves from relational drift by refusing to enter the water—living alone and never committing themselves emotionally to another person. Are we trying to chart the course of lasting relationships when they are simply out of fashion? But it is precisely our claim that a fundamental misunderstanding of the natural course of lasting relationships leads to their premature rupture and creates the very data that underlies the current deep pessimism about them.

This book is above all our response to seeing so many people panic during a natural ebb in the intensity of a loving relationship and, in their despair, precipitate the catastrophic rift that they falsely believe is already there. It is also our response to the cumulative effect of these individual decisions on our collective expectations about marriage and other long-term commitments. Currently, the dominant mood has shifted from romantic dreams to romantic nihilism. The change does not represent a better understanding of the natural course of close relationships. It merely perpetuates an age-old cycle of unreasonable hope and unnecessary cynicism. Riding this see-saw, it is easy to miss the essential cycles that shape the heart of all intimate connections. Romantics and cynics simply draw their evidence from separate sections of an oscillating curve.

Through an extended metaphor of tidal drifts that illuminates both "case histories" and academic research, we have tried to provide a more accurate and complete picture of the course of attachments over time. The picture we have drawn is not completely new. It is not even particularly surprising. It is, however, remarkably hard to hold on to. There is a disconcerting mix of deep sadness and meaningful hope in our description of love and friendship. That emotional complexity creates our third fear. We worry that our book will be misread as an addition to the seemingly endless series of self-help books on the perfectibility of marriage. "Just follow our advice and you can surf the tides safely and happily into a rosy sunset together." The picture of ebb and flow does not provide an end run around the real sorrow and pain that a couple feels when the glorious shared intensity of love is slipping away. The loss is no less real just because it is inevitable and (usually) temporary. The threat of estrangement is no less unsettling. An understanding of the natural motion within a relationship does not erase the sadness during an ebb. All it can do (but this can be crucial) is increase the odds that an ebb *will* be temporary. It does so in three ways. It leads couples to create a regular rhythm of reconnection in their lives so that the inevitable drifts apart do not go on for too long or with no one noticing. It leads couples to value the sound of their "distance alarm" and to take action when drift becomes dangerous. And it prevents couples from committing "marital suicide," a misguided mercy killing that, like true suicide, usually occurs when people cannot imagine that their current pain will ever have a natural end.

Since this pattern is so at odds with our longings and myths, we will run through the bare bones of our argument one last time. In contrast to the simple ideal of constancy in love and friendship, real relationships are always in motion. Cycling between increasing closeness and increasing distance, the motion is much like the ebb and flow of the tides. The cycles are not created by the obvious ways that individuals change and hopefully grow over time. They are a characteristic of the relationship itself. The tidal motion reflects the importance of discovery and unfolding in our experiences of intimacy. Our very success in knowing and loving another person sets the stage for an interval of subtle drift apart. The movement apart can be pulled along by a sense of freshness and novelty attached to a new interest or person. It is regularly pushed by the feeling that something has been lost in the old relationship. That something is given many names—excitement, spark, love itself—but fundamentally what has been lost is the experience of ongoing movement toward even greater intimacy.

Although these movements undermine the ideal of constancy in love and friendship, they have their own stability over time. The drifts apart create the opportunity for rediscovery and the excitement of a new phase of unfolding. Many couples respond intuitively to the weekly or even daily changes in their sense of connection with each other, reserving weekend time for talk and touch that allow their attention and curiosity to shift from the external world back to each other. There are, however, longer cycles extending over months or years that create greater dangers. They are often noticed only after a sense of estrangement has set in, which is not in itself abnormal but easily can be mistaken for the death of love.

In times of less personal freedom, couples were forced to ride out these times and often discovered that circumstance or effort brought about a shift in the tides and a renewal of closeness. Now, without a clear understanding of the natural course of lasting relationships, couples are less likely to stay together long enough to make that discovery. The tidal metaphor leads a couple to make the initial uncomfortable effort to end an episode of estrangement rather than just move on. It helps a couple to attend to the regular rhythm of reconnections in their everyday life rather than to invite uncontrolled drift apart by neglectfully counting on constant love to stand strong against the tides. We grant a necessary importance to currently unfashionable emotions like jealousy and other "distance alarms" that can alert a couple to their increasing estrangement before it becomes irreversible. Finally, we clarify the role of marriage vows and related covenants that both authorize and require each member of a couple to respond to the inevitable drifts apart with an effort to renew closeness rather than a shrug.

The middle chapters examined the (somewhat) predictable phases of married life through the lens of our tidal metaphor. We considered external forces that are likely to trigger or accelerate drift apart and useful strategies for countering that drift. We looked at the effects of children, extended families, work relationships, friendships, sickness, and aging. We addressed gender-based differences in alarms and modes of reconnecting that, for the moment, still shape many relationships. We looked at the way that shared tasks, sex and other forms of touch, conversation, and simple expanses of shared time can restore closeness. We recognized the importance of distance alarms that are responsive enough to signal danger before it is overwhelming but not so sensitive that the smallest ebbs become shattering. The cycles of drift themselves can also be restorative. They let each member of a couple regularly become an object of genuine curiosity for the other, recapturing the precious experience of mutual fascination.

Are we working too hard to provide a model of lasting relationships? Perhaps as life expectancy has increased, we can finally see clearly that the natural life of a loving connection is simply much shorter than the average life span. Even if some couples beat the odds, it might be unrealistic to set that as a goal. Rather than try to ride the tides of love through a lasting relationship, why not accept the naturalness of cycling through multiple relationships in our adult lives?

Barbara Dafoe Whitehead makes a powerful case that we should not because it is bad for our children. She presents compelling evidence that, on any number of measures of success and well-being, children of divorced parents are significantly disadvantaged, no matter how much we might wish that it were not true.[1] A similar argument could be made about individual well-being. In a previous book, we reviewed some of the vast research literature documenting the beneficial effects of social support in general and marriage in particular on physical health and survival.[2] A strong argument can be made that lasting marriage is a remarkably successful and adaptive way of organizing our intimate lives.[3] But statistical arguments are of limited value when decisions are personal, passionate, and invariably focused on specific details that seem to have nothing to do with statistical trends.

We are not naive about either marriage or change. We do not for a moment imagine that the tidal pattern of relationships means that every marriage can and should last. We understand that the cycles of ebb and flow in intimacy do not return a couple to the same place over and over again. They do not leave each individual or the marriage unchanged. The changes can make previously compatible spouses irretrievably unhappy with each other. Remaining within our tidal metaphor, the motion of the tides over time can radically alter the coastline. We were reminded of this fact over the summer, when we walked along a tidal bay toward a small sheltered inlet where, fifteen years before, we had taught our children to swim. The inlet was gone, transformed over the years by tides and storms to a wide cove. The trajectories of two lives, once intertwined, can also unravel and go their separate ways.

Our goal is not to convince people that they should wish to have a lasting relationship. Our goal is to describe in terms that are both vivid and realistic what a lasting relationship looks like over time and how it differs from some of our most deeply held beliefs about love. We offer this description to the many couples who want their connection to last but don't know what to expect or how to improve the odds. We offer it to those (whether professionals, family members, or friends) whose advice can lead a couple to declare a marriage dead or lead them toward renewed closeness. We offer it anyone who wishes to understand the natural course of lasting relationships.

Notes

Introduction

1. Primarily through the work of the psychoanalyst Erik Erikson.

2. William Shakespeare, *The Complete Oxford Shakespeare*, vol. 1, Sonnet 19 (Oxford: Oxford University Press, 1987), 374.

3. David Popenoe and Barbara Dafoe Whitehead, "The State of Our Unions: The Social Health of Marriage in America,"1999. URL: http://marriage.rutgers.edu. The National Marriage Project.

4. Quoted in *Boston Globe*, July 2, 1999.

5. Jerry M. Lewis, "For Better or Worse: Interpersonal Relationships and Individual Outcome," *American Journal of Psychiatry* 155 (1998):582–589.

Chapter 1

1. The only significant exceptions to the universal law of motion are formalized relationships in traditional societies. We will address them in our chapter on friendship.

2. Daniel N. Stern, *The Interpersonal World of the Infant: A View from Psychoanalysis and Developmental Psychology* (New York: Basic Books, 1985), 75.

3. Catherine Schine, *The Evolution of Jane* (Boston: Houghton Mifflin, 1998), 88.

4. Vivian Gornick, "The End of the Novel of Love," in *The End of the Novel of Love*, 157–158 (Boston: Beacon Press, 1997).

5. Jane E. Brody, *New York Times*, July 29, 1992.

6. A two-component model of love fits current research findings, although the same studies also support a single overall entity of love that unites both components. (Michael L. Barnes and Robert J. Sternberg, "A Hierarchical Model of Love and Its Prediction of Satisfaction in Close Relationships," in *Satisfaction in Close Relationships*, ed. Robert J. Sternberg and Mahzad Hojjat [New York: Guilford Press, 1997], 79–101.)

7. P. Tucker and A. Aron, "Passionate Love and Marital Satisfaction at Key Transition Points in the Family Life Cycle," *Journal of Social and Clinical Psychology* 12 (1993): 135–147.

8. R. Contreras, S. S. Hendrick, and C. Hendrick, "Perspectives on Marital Love and Satisfaction in Mexican American and Anglo Couples," *Journal of Counseling and Development* 74 (1996): 408–415.

Chapter 2

1. Peter D. Kramer, *Should You Leave?* (New York: Scribner, 1997).

2. K. Uvnas-Moberg, "Oxytocin May Mediate the Benefits of Positive Social Interaction and Emotions," *Psychoneuroendocrinology* 23 (1998): 819–835.

Chapter 3

1. Donn Byrne and Sarah K Murnen, "Maintaining Loving Relationships," in *The Psychology of Love*, ed. Robert J. Sternberg and Michael L. Barnes (New Haven: Yale University Press, 1988), 299.

2. Gustave Flaubert, *Madame Bovary*, trans. Lowell Blair (New York: Bantam Books, 1981), 34.

3. Ibid.

4. Ibid., 37.

5. Ibid., 37–38.

6. Helen E. Fisher, *Anatomy of Love: The Natural History of Monogamy, Adultery, and Divorce* (New York: W. W. Norton, 1992), 85–86.

7. Ibid., 86–87.

8. Leslie A. Baxter, "A Dialectical Perspective on Communication Strategies in Relationship Development," in *A Handbook of Personal Relationships*, ed. Steve Duck (Chichester: John Wiley and Sons, 1988), 257–273.

9. Timothy Egan, "The Persistence of Polygamy," *New York Times Magazine*, February 28, 1999, 54.

10. Natalie Angier, "Men, Women, Sex and Darwin," *New York Times Magazine*, February 21, 1999, 48.

11. Robert G. Bringle and Bram Buunk, "Examining the Causes and Consequences of Jealousy: Some Recent Findings and Issues," in *The Emerging Field of Personal Relationships*, ed. Robin Gilmour and Steve Duck (Hillsday, N.J.: Lawrence Erlbaum Associates, 1986), 225–240.

12. Karen J. Prager, *The Psychology of Intimacy* (New York: Guilford Press, 1995), 109.

13. Ibid., 20–26.

14. Bringle and Buunk, 320.

15. Quoted in a review by Joseph P. Kahn, *Boston Globe*, February 25, 1999.

16. Prager, 235.

Chapter 4

1. Irving Berlin, "You're Just in Love," *Call Me Madam*, 1950.

2. Sydney Jourard, *The Transparent Self* (New York: Van Nostrand Reinhold, 1971), 32.

3. Leo Tolstoy, *Anna Karenina*, trans. Joel Carmichael (New York: Bantam Books, 1960), 29.

4. Sharon Brehm, "Passionate Love," in *The Psychology of Love*, ed. Robert J. Sternberg and Michael L. Barnes (New Haven: Yale University Press, 1988), 232–263.

5. Ibid.

6. R. N. Bellah, R. Madsen, W. M. Sullivan, A. Swidler, and S. M. Tipton, *Habits of the Heart* (Berkeley, Calif.: University of California Press, 1985), 91.

7. Ibid.

8. Tolstoy, 475.

9. Anthony Walsh, *The Science of Love: Understanding Love and Its Effects on Mind and Body* (Buffalo, N.Y.: Prometheus Books, 1996).

10. Dorothy Tennov, *Love and Limerence: The Experience of Being in Love* (New York: Stein and Day, 1979).

11. Willard Waller, *The Family: A Dynamic Interpretation* (New York: Cordon, 1938), 313.

12. Ted L. Huston, Susan M. McHale, and Ann C. Crouter, "When the Honeymoon's Over: Changes in the Marriage Relationship Over the First Year," in *The Emerging Field of Personal Relationships*, ed. Robin Gilmour and Steve Duck (Hillsdale, N.J.: Lawrence Erlbaum Associates, 1986), 109–132.

13. T. L. Huston and A. F. Chorost, "Behavioral Buffers on the Effect of Negativity on Marital Satisfaction: A Longitudinal Study," *Personal Relationships* 1 (1994): 223–240.

14. John Gottman, *Why Marriages Succeed or Fail* (New York: Simon and Schuster, 1994), 57.

15. Karen J. Prager, *The Psychology of Intimacy* (New York: Guilford Press, 1995), 128.

16. K. Lindahl, M. Clements, and H. Markman, "The Development of Marriage: A Nine-Year Perspective," in *The Developmental Course of Marital Dysfunction*, ed. Thomas N. Bradbury (New York: Cambridge University Press, 1998).

17. A study just published puts the movie back on track, however, by finding evidence for two dips in marital quality, the first after four years and the second after seven years (Lawrence A. Kurdek, "The Nature and Predictors of the Trajectory of Change in Marital Quality for Husbands and Wives Over the First 10 Years of Marriage," *Developmental Psychology* 35 [1999]: 1283–1296).

18. Diane N. Ruble, Alison S. Fleming, Lisa S. Hackel, and Charles Stangor, "Changes in the Marital Relationship During the Transition to Firsttime Motherhood: Effects of Violated Expectations Concerning Division of Household Labor," *Journal of Personality and Social Psychology* 55 (1988): 78–87.

19. Jay Belsky and Emily Pensky, "Marital Change Across the Transition to Parenthood," *Marriage and Family Review* 12 (1988): 133–156.

20. Lynda C. Harriman, "Marital Adjustment as Related to Personal Marital Changes Accompanying Parenthood," *Family Relations: Journal of Applied Family and Child Studies* 35 (1986): 233–239.

21. Prager, 140.

22. Jacqueline Olds, Richard S. Schwartz, Susan Eisen, R. William Betcher, and Anthony Van Niel, "Part-Time Employment and Marital Well-Being: A Hypothesis and Pilot Study," *Family Therapy* 20 (1993): 1–16.

23. See, for example, Juliet Schor, *The Overworked American* (New York: Basic Books, 1992).

Chapter 5

1. Erica Goode, "New Study Finds Middle Age Is Prime of Life," *New York Times*, February 17, 1999.

2. William Kilpatrick, *Why Johnny Doesn't Know Right from Wrong* (New York: Touchstone Books, 1992), 201.

3. Arlie Hochschild, *The Time Bind: When Work Becomes Home and Home Becomes Work* (New York: Metropolitan Books, 1997).

4. Nicholas Lemann, *New York Times Book Review*, May 11, 1997.

5. Louisa May Alcott, *Little Women* (New York: Grosset and Dunlop, 1947), 509.

6. Melinda Marshall, "Sex, Lies and Videotapes: Dying for Time Alone with Your Husband," *Ladies' Home Journal*, May 1999.

7. Jacqueline Olds, Richard S. Schwartz, and Harriet Webster, "Marriage and Other Long-Term Commitments," in *Overcoming Loneliness in Everyday Life* (New York: Birch Lane Press, 1996).

8. Judith A. Feeney, Patricia Noller, and Carla Ward, "Marital Satisfaction and Spousal Interaction," in *Satisfaction in Close Relationships*, ed. Robert J. Sternberg and Mahzad Hojjat (New York: Guilford Press, 1997), 160–189.

9. E. Langer and J. Rodin, "The Effects of Enhanced Personal Responsibility among the Aged: A Field Experiment in an Institutional Setting," *Journal of Personality and Social Psychology* 34 (1976): 191–198.

10. Thomas Moore, *Care of the Soul* (New York: Harper Perennial, 1992).

Chapter 6

1. Irvin D. Yalom, *Existential Psychotherapy* (New York: Basic Books, 1980), 174.

2. N. Stinnett, L. M. Carter, and J. E. Montgomery, "Older Persons' Perceptions of Their Marriages," *Journal of Marriage and the Family* 32 (1972):428–434.

3. C. L. Johnson, "The Impact of Illness on Late-Life Marriages," *Journal of Marriage and the Family* 47 (1985): 165–172.

4. Marie-Louise Mares and Mary Anne Fitzpatrick, "The Aging Couple," in *Handbook of Communication and Aging Research*, ed. Jon F. Nussbaum and Justine Coupland (Mahwah, N.J.: Lawrence Erlbaum Associates, 1995), 185–205.

5. T. Caplow, H. M. Bahr, B. A. Chadwick, R. Hill, and M. H. Williamson, *The Middletown Families* (Minneapolis: University of Minnesota Press, 1982), 117.

6. C. Cole, "Marital Quality in Later Life," in *Independent Aging: Family and Social Systems Perspectives*, ed. W. Quinn and G. Hughston (Rockville, Md.: Aspen Systems, 1984), 72–90.

7. R. Gilford, "Contrasts in Marital Satisfaction Throughout Old Age: An Exchange Theory Analysis, *Journal of Gerontology* 39 (1984): 325–333.

8. D. H. Olson, "Family Types, Family Stress and Family Satisfaction : A Family Development Perspective," in *Family Transitions*, ed. C. J. Falicov (New York: Guilford Press, 1988), 55–80.

9. Ibid., 166.

10. Richard B. Miller, Karla Hemesath, and Briana Nelson, "Marriage in Middle and Later Life," in *The Aging Family: New Visions in Theory, Practice, and Reality*, ed. Terry D. Hargrave and Suzanne Midori Hanna (New York: Brunner Mazel, 1997), 178–198.

11. E. H. Newberger, R. L. Hampton, T. J. Marx, and K. M. White, "Child Abuse and Pediatric Social Illness: An Epidemiological Analysis and Ecological Reformulation," *Americal Journal of Orthopsychiatry* 56 (1986): 598–601.

12. N. C. Keating and P. Cole, "What Do I Do with Him 24 Hours a Day? Changes in the Housewife Role After Retirement," *The Gerontologist* 20 (1980): 84–89.

13. G. R. Lee and C. L. Shehan, "Retirement and Marital Satisfaction," *Journal of Gerontology* 44 (1989): S226-S230.

14. Much more intriguing but beside the point for our present discussion, individuals with depression do not fool themselves in this way. Though depressive thought is clearly less adaptive than nondepressive thought, it is at times more realistic. For a summary of research on depressive and normal cognition, see Richard S. Schwartz, "Mood Brighteners, Affect Tolerance and the Blues," *Psychiatry* 54 (1991): 397–403.

15. Bronislaw Malinowski, "Magic, Science and Religion," in *Magic, Science and Religion and Other Essays* (New York: Doubleday Anchor, 1954), 53.

16. Stephen L. Carter, "The Insufficiency of Honesty," *Atlantic Monthly*, February 1996, 74–46.

17. John Bayley, *Elegy for Iris* (New York: St. Martin's Press, 1999), 213.

18. Ibid., 160.

19. Ibid., 265.

20. Ibid., 267.

21. Ibid., 44.

22. Ibid., 123.

23. Ibid., 258–259.

24. Ibid., 235.

25. Mares and Fizpatrick.

26. Ibid., 195.

27. M. Kovar, "Elderly People: The Population 65 Years and Over," in *Health: The United States 1976–1977* (U.S. Departmment of Education and Welfare Publication No. HRA 77–1232) (Washington, D.C.: U.S. Government Printing Office, 1977).

28. Johnson.

29. S. Weishaus and D. Field, "A Half Century of Marriage: Continuity or Change?" *Journal of Marriage and the Family* 50 (1988): 763–774.

30. Benjamin Franklin, *The Autobiography of Benjamin Franklin and Selections from His Writings* (New York: Random House, 1944), 115.

31. R. Stone, G. L. Cafferata, and J. Sangl, "Caregivers of the Frail Elderly: A National Profile," *Gerontologist* 27 (1987): 616–626.

32. Philip Roth, *Patrimony: A True Story* (New York: Touchstone, 1991), 175.

33. L. K. Wright, "The Impact of Alzheimer's Disease on the Marital Relationship," *Gerontologist* 31 (1991): 224–237.

34. S. Zarit, P. Todd, and J. Zarit, "Subjective Burden of Husbands and Wives as Caregivers: A Longitudinal Study," *Gerontologist* 26 (1986): 260–266.

35. P. Uhlenberg, T. Cooney, and R. Boyd, "Divorce for Women After Midlife," *Journal of Gerontology* 45 (1990): S3-S11.

36. Bayley, 73.

Chapter 7

1. "Add Health Findings Released," American Sociological Association *Footnotes*, September/October 1997, 1.

2. Lawrence Steinberg, *Beyond the Classroom: Why School Reform Has Failed and What Parents Need to Do* (New York: Simon and Schuster, 1996).

Chapter 8

1. John Bowlby, *Attachment*, vol. 1 of *Attachment and Loss* (New York: Basic Books, 1969), *Separation: Anxiety and Anger*, vol. 2 of *Attachment and Loss* (New York: Basic Books, 1973), and *Loss: Sadness and Depression*, vol. 3 of *Attachment and Loss* (New York: Basic Books, 1980).

2. If this progression sounds familiar but out of context, that is because Elizabeth Kübler-Ross later developed a similar but much better known schema for an individual's response to the threat of a fatal illness.

3. Daniel N. Stern, *The Interpersonal World of the Infant: A View from Psychoanalysis and Developmental Psychology* (New York: Basic Books, 1985), 75.

4. John Bowlby, *The Making and Breaking of Affectional Bonds* (London: Tavistock, 1979), 69.

5. M. D. S. Ainsworth, M. C. Blehar, E. Waters, and S. Wall, *Patterns of Attachment: A Psychological Study of the Strange Situation* (Hillsdale, N.J.: Erlbaum, 1978).

6. Phillip Shaver, Cindy Hazan, and Donna Bradshaw, "Love as Attachment: The Integration of Three Behavioral Systems," in *The Psychology of Love*, ed. Robert J. Sternberg and Michael L. Barnes (New Haven: Yale University Press, 1988), 68–99.

7. Ibid.

8. Ibid.

9. Lydia Flem, *Casanova: The Man Who Really Loved Women*, trans. Catherine Temerson (New York: Farrar Straus Giroux, 1997), 13.

10. Ibid., 139.

11. Ibid., 140.

12. Early psychoanalytic theories led Freud to refer to mental representations of people as objects and the unfortunate term stuck.

13. Richard S. Schwartz, "Mood Brighteners, Affect Tolerance, and the Blues," *Psychiatry* 54 (1991): 397–403.

Chapter 9

1. John Bayley, *Elegy for Iris* (New York: St. Martin's Press, 1999), 8–9.

2. Stacey J. Oliker, *Best Friends and Marriage: Exchange Among Women* (Berkeley, Calif.: University of California Press, 1989).

3. Nancy Chodorow, *The Reproduction of Mothering: Psychoanalysis and the Sociology of Gender* (Berkeley, Calif.: University of California Press, 1978).

4. S. Rose and F. C. Serafica, "Keeping and Ending Casual, Close, and Best Friendships," *Journal of Social and Personal Relationships* 3 (1986): 275–288.

5. Oliker, 29.

6. Ibid., 29.

7. Ibid., 30.

8. For example, Claude S. Fischer, Robert M. Jackson, Ann Steuve, Katherine Gerson, and Lynn M. Jones, *Networks and Places: Social Relations in the Urban Setting* (New York: Free Press, 1977).

9. M. Argyle and M. Henderson, "The Rules of Friendship," *Journal of Social and Personal Relationships* 1 (1984): 211–237.

10. Oliker, 57.

11. David Schneider, *American Kinship: A Cultural Account* (Englewood Cliffs, N.J.: Prentice-Hall, 1968), 54.

12. Ibid.

13. M. B. Parlee, "The Friendship Bond," *Psychology Today*, October 1979, 42–54.

14. Oliker, 56.

15. Ibid., 57.

16. Ibid., 123.

17. Ibid., 58.

18. See summary in Jacqueline Olds, Richard S. Schwartz, and Harriet Webster, *Overcoming Loneliness in Everyday Life* (New York: Birch Lane Press, 1996), 42–44.

19. Olds, Schwartz, Eisen, Betcher, and Van Niel.

20. E. Schein, *Organizational Psychology* (Englewood Cliffs, N.J.: Prentice-Hall, 1965), 108.

Chapter 10

1. Nicholas Sparks, *The Notebook* (New York: Warner Books, 1996).

2. David Popenoe and Barbara Dafoe Whitehead: "The State of Our Unions: The

Social Health of Marriage in America," 1999. URL: http://marriage.rutgers.edu. The National Marriage Project.

3. Ibid.

4. Barbara Dafoe Whitehead, *The Divorce Culture: Rethinking Our Commitments to Marriage and Family* (New York: Vintage Books, 1998), 38.

5. E. J. Graff, *What Is Marriage For?* (Boston: Beacon Press, 1999), ix-x.

6. Ibid.

7. Whitehead, 53.

8. J. Randall Nichols, *Ending Marriage, Keeping Faith: A New Guide Through the Spiritual Journey of Divorce* (New York: Crossroad Publishing, 1991), 63.

9. Whitehead, 91–106.

10. Glenn T. Stanton, *Why Marriage Matters: Reasons to Believe in Marriage in Postmodern Society* (Colorado Springs, Colo.: Pinon Press, 1997).

11. Jacqueline Olds, Richard S. Schwartz, and Harriet Webster, *Overcoming Loneliness in Everyday Life* (New York: Birch Lane Press, 1996), 32–47.

12. Robert T. Michael, John H. Gagnon, Edward O. Laumann, and Gina Kolata, *Sex in America: A Definitive Survey* (Boston: Little, Brown, and Company, 1994), 1, 131.

13. Edward O. Laumann, John H. Gagnon, Robert T. Michael, and Stuart Michaels, *The Social Organization of Sexuality: Sexual Practices in the United States* (Chicago: University of Chicago Press, 1994), 121.

14. Julie E. Ginsburg, "A Lawyer's Brief: No Such Thing as an Easy Divorce," *Boston Globe*, May 25, 1999.

15. Olds, Schwartz, and Webster, 26–27.

16. Whitehead, 5.

17. Whitehead, 13.

Chapter 11

1. John Gottman, *Why Marriages Succeed or Fail . . . and How You Can Make Yours Last* (New York: Fireside, 1995), 127.

2. Arlie Russell Hochschild, *The Time Bind: When Work Becomes Home and Home Becomes Work* (New York: Metropolitan Books,1997).

3. Ibid., 198.

4. Juliet B. Schor, *The Overworked American: The Unexpected Declilne of Leisure* (New York: Basic Books, 1992), 35.

5. William S. Pollack, *Real Boys: Rescuing Our Sons from the Myths of Boyhood* (New York: Random House, 1998).

Chapter 12

1. Barbara Dafoe Whitehead, *The Divorce Culture: Rethinking Our Commitments to Marriage and Family* (New York: Alfred A. Knopf, 1997).

2. Jacqueline Olds, Richard S. Schwartz, and Harriet Webster, "The Hazards of Loneliness," chap. 4 in *Overcoming Loneliness in Everyday Life* (New York: Birch Lane Press, 1996).

3. For example, Glenn T. Stanton, *Why Marriage Matters: Reasons to Believe in Marriage in Postmodern Society* (Colorado Springs: Pinon Press, 1997).

Index